WARNING:

Have you ever answered YES to any of the following?

- Are you perpetually rumpled, dirty, unclean, unshaven, unkempt, perhaps even STINKY — in public — and find that you simply don't care?

- As a parent, have you started to resemble Chewbacca? Make Wookie noises?

- Do you find yourself scarfing cold greasy kid-food while standing up/walking/running/crying?

- Has your memory... um, is the... what was the question?

- Have you come into contact with blood, vomit, feces, urine, hair, or smooshed food all within five minutes?

- Have you ever caught barf? *Someone else's* barf?

- Have you ever threatened to call Santa? The Easter Bunny? The Tooth Fairy? The FBI Crime Lab? All four?

- Do you ever find yourself replacing curse words with nonsense words that sound the same? (e.g., "BOB SAGET!!")

- Have you ever hidden *Goodnight Moon* in the freezer?

If you answered **YES** to any/all of the above questions, then we WELCOME you to...

☯
THE TAO OF DA-DA

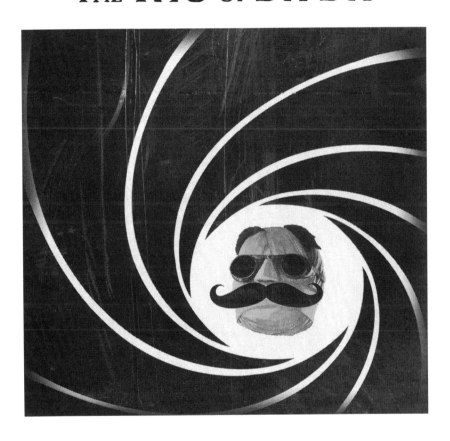

The TAO of DA-DA

or

Strong Winds CAN *Blow All Day Depending on How Much Sugar Has Been Ingested*

by

Gary Clemenceau

(aka, A Man Called Da-da)

*Void where prohibited
Your future may vary -- a lot*

The Printed Voice

Novato, California

*For Da-da's boys,
Bronko & Nagurski
and, of course,* Ma-ma
*who outranks us all,
even without a mustache*

Other Books by Gary Clemenceau:

Banker's Holiday: A Novel of Fiscal Irregularity

*The TORPOMETRONOMICON:
10 Years of AcmeVaporware Miscommunications*

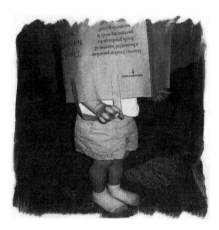

The following is a work of satire and parody, take your pick,
based on a public domain translation of *The Tao te Ching*.
Da-da has the greatest respect for *The Tao*, as you'll see.
All text, original photographs and transformative illustrations
© Copyright Gary Clemenceau. All rights reserved.
No portion of this book may be reproduced without permission.
Original photographs available on request.
No part of the following material may be reproduced
without written permission of the author, or his publisher
who is a very nice lady, when unprovoked.

*The TAO of Da-da (or, "Strong Winds CAN Blow All Day
Depending on How Much Sugar's Been Ingested")*
By Gary Clemenceau (aka, A Man Called Da-da)
Published by The Printed Voice
PO Box 1071
Novato, CA 94948
www.lesliekeenan.com/printed-voice/
ISBN-10 09891661-9-8
ISBN-13 978-0-9891661-9-5

CONTENTS

The Tao of Da-da (Stanzas 1-82)   pp 15-85
Addendum: Miscellaneous Da-da   pp 179-195
The *Other* Addendum: Postmodern Carols   pp 197-261

FOREWORD

Most forewords go in reverse. This one is no different, though it could be said to be upside-down and backwards. Regardless of direction, it's necessary to offer a bit of explanation into the dreaded "Da-da mindset" before one ventures too far into Da-da's brackish Third-Person parenting waters.

What's Da-da talking about? Put simply, women are usually better than men at being designated, stay-at-home-parents. Why? Well, besides being better at multi-tasking than males, women have also been *dealing with males* (and other females) for years prior to being saddled with children... and since men often act like children, parenting isn't that big of a stretch for females.

Men on the other hand have to deal with all sorts of conflicting emotions when donning the mantle of "Mr. Mom" or "Stay-at-Home-Dad," a mantle which is indeed made of solid gold, but gold that gets hotter and heavier the moment you stop moving. Good or bad, everything seems upside down and backwards these days. Banks have no money. Politicians have no polity. Brown is the new orange. And most importantly for those holding this book: men are the new women, and vice versa. It's a world gone mad, but at least it's interesting.

Now a note on tone.

Da-da wrote these stanzas, based on a public domain translation of *The Tao te Ching*, while neck-deep in the parenting trenches, laden as he was with two sumo-wrestler boys, aged zero to infinity. This means Da-da was both happy and sad, horrified and angry, insane and jolly pretty much all at the same time. Da-da laughed, he cried, he was on the edge of his seat. This hasn't changed much.

After reading the stanzas contained in the first half of *TAO*, you may begin to see the moment when Da-da truly lost it. You may also see where Da-da *found* it again, if he actually ever did, in the second half. Sure, desperation settled in, took a chair, and stayed all winter, but this taught Da-da the value of humor in long-term suffering (which he'd of course learned before, but had blissfully forgotten till he had children), because without humor, we all start to look like Dick Cheney. (If you're a desperate, stinky and unshaven parent and you'd like to know where you stand at this very moment, try taking the "Da-da Trench Test" on p. 185.)

Having recently passed through the raging rapids of The Early Da-da years (as they've become known), Da-da is currently doing lots of bailing and delousing, getting as much existential water and barnacles off the family boat as possible before venturing into deeper currents and more turbulent (teen) waters and... well, Da-da may one day renounce the Third Person, but you never know; Second Person seems to be all Da-da can hope for at this point. And before Da-da leaves you, it should also be most strenuously noted that:

> *This small volume serves as the surest form*
> *of literary birth control yet in existence.*

Best of luck in all your future parenting endeavors. The human race is counting on you.

~ Gary Clemenceau

(aka, A Man Called Da-da)
Void where prohibited
Your future may vary — a lot

ONE

The Man Called Da-da that can be told
is not the Eternal Da-da.
The mess that can be cleaned
is not the Eternal Mess.

The unstoppable child is the eternally real.
The naming of the unstoppable child is the origin
of all pain and suffering.

Free from children, you realize the mystery.
Caught by children, you see only the manifestation.

Yet mystery and manifestation
arise from the same source.
This source is called, "Ma-ma."

Ma-ma within darkness:
the gateway to all understanding
about why Da-da did this to himself in the first place.

TWO

When people see some children as beautiful
other children become ugly.
When people see some children as good
other children become bad.

Being childlike and childish create each other.
Difficult and easy live on the same street.
Long and short are your hours and days off, respectively.
High and low depend on days Ma-ma has off.
Before- and after-naps follow each other over and over again
until you die, then repeat.

Therefore a Man Called Da-da
acts without doing anything
and teaches without saying anything
mostly because no one listens to him.
Things arise and he lets them come.
Like he has any choice?
Things disappear and he lets them go
as they're probably inside the couch.

He has but doesn't possess
acts but doesn't expect
hears but blocks it out
as much as he can this side of a beer keg.
When his work is done, he forgets it.
He couldn't remember it, anyway.
That is why his work lasts forever.
Shh. Don't wake him.

THREE

If you overesteem great parents
Da-da becomes powerless.
If you overvalue the power of television
children begin to zombify.

A Man Called Dada leads
by emptying his mind
and filling children's tummies;
by weakening his ambition
and toughening children's resolve.
He helps children gain everything
they know, understand everything they feel
and creates confusion
in himself until he realizes that
his life is basically over as he knows it
so he should stop worrying
and take up fishing
if only in his mind.

Practice doing everything
and everything will fall into place…
because that's probably where you left it.

FOUR

A Man Called Da-da is like an old well:
used, and mostly used up;
pissed on, barfed on
and filled with garbage.
He is like the eternal void:
filled with nothing of consequence
save for the faint echo of infinite possibilities.

He is hidden, but always present.
No one wants to look at him —
not with that Furby hair.
And c'mon, he's wearing faded tie-dye
and hasn't shaved in weeks.
No one knows who gave birth to him
(except his mother, who's laughing in a corner)
but he has a certain look about him:
he looks older than God.

FIVE

A Man Called Da-da doesn't take sides.
Both sides are equally guilty.
He doesn't take sides. (Didn't Da-da just say that?)
He just wants quiet.

A Man Called Da-da is like a bellows:
he is empty, yet full of hot air.
The more you test him, the more hot air he produces;
the more you talk to him, the less you understand.

Hold on to the center.
Da-da's got the ball.
Or he *is* the ball.

SIX

A Man Called Da-da is often called Mr. Mom:
an oxymoron if Da-da ever saw one.
He is not a Mister, and he is not Mom,
but something somewhere in between.
He is empty yet exhaustible;
his former Mister suit is big,
but Ma-ma's shoes are bigger.
Still, Da-da gives birth to infinite Da-da worlds
of screaming and laughter
somewhere between Christmas
and that trip to the emergency room.

He is always present when you barf
especially when it's all over him.
Feel free to use him any way you want.
Da-da is super-absorbent.

SEVEN

A Man Called Da-da is infinite, eternal.
Why is he eternal?
He isn't.
Just makes him feel better when you say it.
He was never born;
thus, he can never die,
until his work is done...
which is never.
Why is he infinite?
He isn't.
But he can hear what you
and your brother are doing.
He has no desires for himself
save for sleep.
By himself.
In a five-star hotel.
With clean white sheets.
Thus is he present for all people, big and small
but especially for room service people.

A Man Called Da-da stays behind
to clean up the mess,
that is why he's ahead.
Actually, he isn't ahead
but... well, you know.
In reality, he's detached from all fun things;
that is why he's one without them.
Because he's let go of himself
he's perfectly fulfilled
provided he gets some sleep.

EIGHT

The supreme good is like water
which nourishes all things without trying to.
It is content with the low places that people disdain.
Thus, it is like A Man Called Da-da.

In dwelling, live close to the ground.
If you live too high, you might be tempted to spy
on the neighbors.
In thinking, keep to the simple:
like Da-da, you might not have any choice.
In conflict, be fair and generous:
or at least fake it well.
In governing, don't try to control:
people will only laugh at you.
In work, do what you enjoy:
children like being taped to the wall.
In family life, run like hell.

Remember:
when you are content to run like hell
and don't compare or compete
everyone will respect you.
You are sane!

NINE

Fill their bowls to the brim
and they will spill
and *you* will have to clean it up.
Keep sharpening your knife
and it will blunt
against all those boxes of macaroni and cheese.
Chase after money and security
and your heart will giggle like a little girl
at your folly.
Care about people's approval of your tie-dye and beard
and you will be their prisoner.

Do your work, then step back.
The only path to serenity
is in fearlessly wearing the tie-dye and beard.

32 *Gary Clemenceau, or A Man Called Da-da*

TEN

Can you coax the Small Beings' minds from wandering
and keep to the original oneness? Or perhaps twoness?
No.
Can you let their bodies become
strong and supple by plying them with "balanced meals"
they will never eat?
No.
Can you cleanse their inner vision
from that horrible commercial they just accidently saw?
Maybe with a lot of Scooby Doo.
Can you love children and lead them
without imposing your will?
Don't be silly.
Can you deal with the most vital matters
by letting events take their course?
Cover your ears, jump out of the way and find out.
Can you step back from you own mind
and thus understand all things?
Of course not.

Giving birth and nourishing,
having without possessing,
acting with no expectations,
leading and not trying to control:
these are all impossible for A Man Called Da-da
but don't tell anyone, even if it is the Supreme Virtue.
When in doubt, take down your pants
and slide on the ice.

ELEVEN

We install training wheels and provide the training
but it is A Man Called Da-da
who makes the bike move.

We constantly fill the sippy cup
but it is the emptiness inside
that cannot ever be filled.

We hammer our thumb for a house
but it is the inner and outer expletives
that make the moment livable.

We work without a net
so falling on our faces
is what we deserve.

36 *Gary Clemenceau, or A Man Called Da-da*

TWELVE

Toy colors blind the eye.
Screaming screams deafen the ear.
Chicken nuggets numb the taste.
Lack of thought weakens the mind.
Desires would wither the heart
if we had the energy for desires.

A Man Called Da-da observes the world
but trusts his little television in the garage.
He allows things to come and go
because he cannot possibly control them.
His heart is open as the sky
during his quadruple bypass.

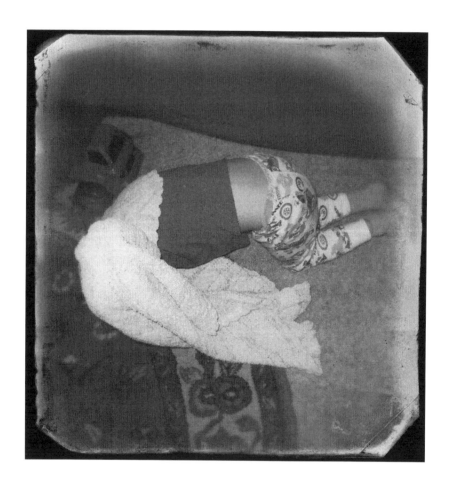

THIRTEEN

Success is as dangerous as failure.
Hope is as hollow as fear.
These things are far beyond A Man Called Da-da.

What does it mean that success is as dangerous as failure?
If you go up the ladder
your position is shaky.
When you stand with your two feet on the ground
you stand a better chance of catching the barf.

What does it mean that hope is as hollow as fear?
Hope and fear are both phantoms
that arise from thinking of "spare time."
When we don't see the self as necessary to anything
but finding The Blankie
what do we have to fear?
We fear NOT finding The Blankie.

See the world as your Bankie.
Have faith in the way it smells and constantly gets torn.
Love The Blankie as your self
but wash it a lot more;
then you can stop caring for all things.

FOURTEEN

Look for the toy, and it can't be seen.
Listen for the toy, and it can't be heard.
Reach for the toy, and it can't be grasped...
toy avalanche.

Above, it isn't bright
below, it isn't dark
buried under toys in the infinite closet.
Seamless, unnameable...
Da-da returns to the realm of nothingness.
Toy form that includes all toy forms;
dinosaur image that strangely looks like Da-da;
a subtle glow-in-the-dark skeleton beyond all conception.
Da-da as lost toy.
A little help.

Approach Da-da and there is no beginning;
follow Da-da into the toy closet and there is no end.
You can't know it, but you're hosed —
lost in your own Da-da life.
Just realize where you come from
and where you're stuck, indefinitely.
Then crack open a beer and get over it.
This is the essence of Da-da wisdom.

FIFTEEN

The Ancient Da-da Masters were profound and subtle,
their wisdom unfathomable
probably because they didn't talk much.
There is no way to describe it;
all we can describe is their appearance:
old, grey, spent.

They were more careful
when someone splashed in the puddles,
alert as a chicken in enemy territory.
Courteous as a ninja.
Fluid as a leaky sippy cup.
Immutable as a block of Play Doh.
Receptive as a block of Play Doh.
Clear as a block of Play Doh.

Do you have the patience to wait
till your mud settles and the water is clear?
Can you remain unmoving
till the right action arises by itself?
Of course not.
Someone somewhere is screaming.

A Man Called Da-da doesn't seek fulfillment.
He's too numb.
Not seeking, not expecting,
he is present
and welcomes all things carbonated.

The Ancient Da-da Masters laugh.

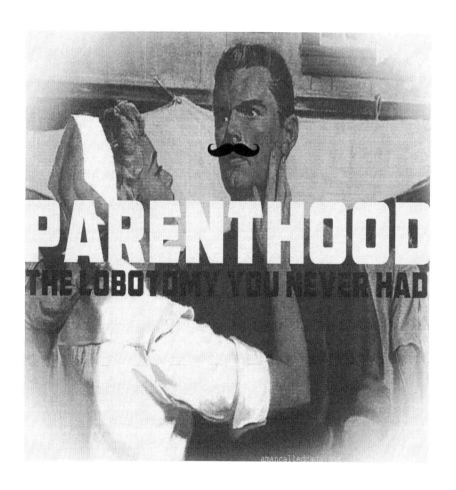

SIXTEEN

Empty your mind of all thoughts.
Like you had any left?
Let your heart be at peace
but try to stay conscious.
Watch the turmoil born of Small Beings
but only contemplate using the duct tape.

Each separate being in the universe
returns to a common Source.
Returning to the Source is serenity,
but only after the Small Beings leave for school.

If you don't realize this,
you stumble in confusion and sorrow
and wonder why you ever let Ma-ma talk you into this.
When you realize that this life is like
hitting yourself in the head with a ball peen hammer
and that it feels really good when you stop,
you naturally become tolerant of hitting yourself in the head
with ball peen hammers;
disinterested, amused, bruised —
shellshocked as a WWI grandfather,
dignified as a trussed chicken, you are
immersed in the stupified wonder that is A Man Called Da-da.
You think you can deal with whatever life brings you,
but you're so wrong.
And when death comes, you are so ready.
But don't get cocky.
Da-da comes back as The Living Dead.
The only real trouble is in recognizing the difference.

SEVENTEEN

When Da-da governs, the Small Beings
with their Ten Thousand Things
are hardly aware he exists.
After all, he's not Ma-ma.
Next best is the Da-da who is loved,
because he let's them watch Pink Panther all day.
Next is the Da-da who is feared,
because he makes the Loud Noise.
Best is the Da-da who is despised,
because he won't let them watch Pink Panther all day.
In this case, don't turn your back on the Small Beings:
Pink Panther is powerful.

If you don't trust the Small Beings,
you make them untrustworthy.
This is because they ARE untrustworthy,
especially around fire and balloons and tape
and broken glass and…
well, it's a long list.

A Man Called Da-da doesn't talk, he acts.
When his work is done,
the Small Beings say,
"LOOK, Da-da! We made this for you!"

— **SPLAT** —

[sigh]

Da-da's work is never done.

EIGHTEEN

When A Man Called Da-da is not around,
goodness and piety will appear.
Figures.

When Small Beings' intelligence declines,
cleverness and knowledge step forth, usually from Da-da.
When there is no peace in the family,
forced filial hugginess begins.
When the house falls into utter chaos,
cleanliness is born.
Yeah, right.

A Man Called Da-da needs his illusions.
They're all he's got left.

NINETEEN

Throw away holiness and wisdom
and Small Beings may run amok like headless chickens.
Throw away morality and justice
and Small Beings may do the right thing (not).
Throw away industry and profit
and you have A Man Called Da-da.

If these three aren't enough
just stay at the center of the circle
and let the dodgeball do its job.

TWENTY

Stop thinking about kids' soccer and end your troubles.
What difference between goal and no goal?
What difference between success and failure?
Must you value what others value and YELL
about driving the ball all the time?

Some people are constantly excited
as though they were at a soccer match
because life, they say, is like a soccer match
just scaled way down, with a lot less excitement
and cheaper T-shirts and beer.

Meanwhile, Da-da sits in the stands.
He alone is expressionless — primarily because
two of the players woke Da-da up at 2:30 this morning
playing with Da-da's alarm clock again.
So, Da-da sits, head full of concrete, like a
motionless white-and-black roundish thing:
Da-da is the Unkicked Ball.

Other people have what they need.
Their children SCORE! and do the scoring dance.
Da-da alone possesses nothing. Why?
Because he has children who aren't driving the ball all the time.
But they're really good at Legos.

When forced to play, Da-da drifts about the field
muttering like someone without a home.
He is like an idiot... a lot of the time, but not always.
Ok, most of the time
but his opposing net is often unguarded.

Other people are bright, colorful.
Da-da alone is dark, drab.
Other people are sharp.
Da-da alone is dull.
Maybe Da-da needs a new uniform.

Da-da is different from ordinary people.
He embraces his limp lack of coordination.
Having passed this lack to his children, we huddle and scheme;
our thick, black-rimmed glasses mark us and
show us the way to the library
where we learn to write of OPG (Other People's Goals).

TWENTY ONE

A Man Called Da-da keeps his mind — what's left of it —
always at one with the to-do list, or
THE LIST as it's known,
the completion of which gives Ma-ma radiance.
Ma-ma is all about radiance.

A Man Called Da-da sees
THE LIST
tacked on the Refrigerator of Destiny every morning.
How can he not see it? It's BIG.
And how the hell can he be at one with something so BIG?

He can't, of course.
He can only cope with its omnipresent enormity
by not clinging to ideas.
This is easy for Da-da.
Da-da doesn't have any ideas.

A Man Called Da-da is dark and unfathomable
because all his neurons have been burnt
by the Ten Thousand Small and Noisy Things.
But how, O HOW, can he make Ma-ma radiant?
He can do everything on THE LIST.

Since before time and space,
Da-da has had THE LIST.
It is beyond do and do not.
How does he know this is true?
He looks inside and sees Ma-ma giving him THE LOOK.

TWENTY TWO

If you want to find your Blankie,
look where you left it.
If you want Da-da to be happy,
get Buzz Lightyear off the cat.
If you want to become full,
eat your damn dinner.
If you want to be reborn,
be Da-da's guest:
if you want to be given everything
you might want to find a different family.

A Man Called Da-da, by residing in this "Da-da-ness"
sets an example for all Da-da People.
Because he doesn't display himself,
his skin grows pale.
Because he has nothing of his own,
the Small Beings can play with anything they want.
Because he doesn't know who he is,
Big People put him in the psych ward.
Because he has no goal in mind,
the goalie will always succeed.

When the Ancient Da-da Masters said
"If you want to be given everything,
then pack your bags"
they weren't just using empty phrases:
The Ancient Da-da Masters were pissed.
Never piss off the Ancient Da-da Masters.

TWENTY THREE

Express yourself completely.
Speak up — then be quiet.
Be like the forces of nature:
when it blows, there is only wind;
when it rains, there is only rain;
when your brother hits you, don't scream.
The clouds will pass, the sun will shine through.
There will be time to get even.

If you open yourself to The Tao of Da-da
you are at one with the Da-da
and can embody him completely in the Third Person.
If you open yourself to doing what Da-da asks
THE FIRST TIME HE ASKS IT
you are at one with the dessert,
and you can play Minecraft till the dawn.
If you open yourself to yelling,
you are at one with the yelling,
and you can accept it completely
alone in your room.

Open yourself to The Tao of Da-da
and do everything Da-da asks
THE FIRST TIME HE ASKS IT
and Santa will fall into place.

TWENTY FOUR

He who stands on tiptoe on top of the stool,
winds up in the Emergency Room.
He who rushes ahead,
gets tripped by the cat.
He who tries to shine —
better not do it with matches.
He who defines himself with The Screaming Chicken
will spend time in solitary.
He who has power over others,
will attend sensitivity training.
He who clings to his Blankie,
will eventually make it into a stinky rag of a sport coat.

If you want to be in accord with The Tao of Da-da
close your mouth, clean up your room, and be safe.

TWENTY FIVE

There was something quiet and perfect
before the Small Beings were born.
All was serene, empty of the Ten Thousand Things
that now lie scattered all over the house.
Things were solitary.
Unchanging.
NICE.
Pillows stayed on the sofa: infinite, eternally present.
Then Ma-ma became Ma-ma and changed all this.
Da-da had nothing to do with it, honestly.
He just lives here.

When the Small Beings are in school,
echoes of this past solitude flow through all things
inside and out, and return again and again
to mock A Man Called Da-da.

Don't get Da-da wrong.

The Small Beings are great.
Ma-ma is great.
The Ten-Thousand-Thing Debris Field is great.
SpongeBob is great.
These are the four great powers.
A Man Called Da-da is way way at the back of the bus.
But the new order of things is intriguing.
The Small Beings follow the Ma-ma.
The Ma-ma brings home the bacon.
A Man Called Da-da fries it up in a pan with some onions
removes the bacon, adds burger and green peppers
a tablespoon of chili powder, a bit of cumin, salt & pepper.
Meanwhile, he boils bowtie pasta al dente and
mixes it all with quarter-inch chunks of cheddar cheese

and a big can of stewed tomatoes;
bakes it for about an hour at 375 degrees
and serves it up: Da-da Bowtie Goulash.
Later, A Man Called Da-da follows behind
cleaning up the empty dishes.

Serenity and quiet reign once again,
except now there are leftovers (that no one will eat).

TWENTY SIX

The heavy foot is the root of the Red Light Ticket.
The unmoved refuses to put his shoes on and go to school.

Thus, A Man Called Da-da travels all day
without leaving home.
Later, while running errands,
the splendid views out his windshield
stay serenely in place, mocking Da-da
with thoughts of dry cleaning, shoe repair, grocery lists…
and, of course cleaning, power washing, scraping and painting
the Mortgaged Container of the Ten Thousand Things.

Why should a demi-lord of the manor
flit about like a fool?
If you let yourself be blown to and fro,
you lose touch with your root.
If you let restlessness move you,
you lose touch with who you are.
Then again, try explaining that to Ma-ma.

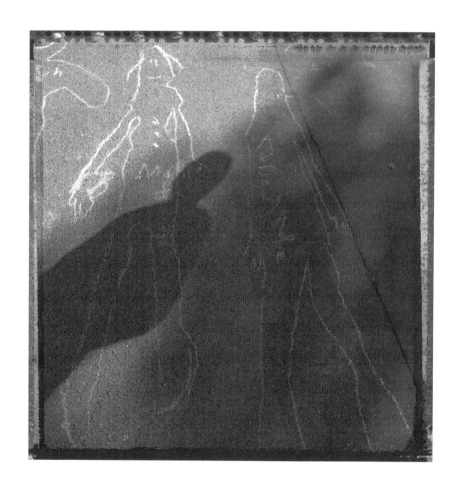

TWENTY SEVEN

A good Da-da has no fixed plans
and is not intent on arriving on time —
yet he does, despite being late.
A better Da-da lets his intuition lead him
away from the Ten Thousand Things scattered all over the house.
A great Da-da has freed himself of desire,
gotten everything done way in advance,
and keeps his mind open to the completeness of a good burrito.

Thus, does A Man Called Da-da maintain
lots of time for Small Beings
without rejecting anyone, regardless of how
much jelly is on their face.
He is ready to use all situations as future lessons
and doesn't waste that trip to the Emergency Room.
That long bone inserted in the skin of his chest
at the beginning of parenthood —
the one he's been hanging from for years, see?
it will feel SO GOOD when it's removed one day
far way in the future
when his kids leave for college, drop out and
marry that circus performer.
After that, there's the sofa
and college football for him to enjoy
for about an hour before he's dead.
And of course free Cirque du Soleil tickets.
This is called The Triumph of A Man Called Da-da.

What is a good Da-da, but a bad Da-da's teacher?
What is a bad Da-da, but a good Da-da
without poetic summation?
Doesn't sound right, but what the hell.
If you don't understand this, you will get lost
however intelligent you are

somewhere in the foggy Da-da-ness of
A Man Called Da-da.
It is the great secret.

What is the great secret?
Da-da can't remember.
His mind is gone.
Pass the remote.

TWENTY EIGHT

Know the female
and you might get scale models;
and once you receive that Small Being in your arms,
don't forget to duck:
projectile vomit
often has your name on it.

Know the clean
yet embrace the unclean:
it's gonna happen no matter what
and, unlike your furniture, your hands are washable.
If you embrace this pattern for your world,
the spirit of A Man Called Da-da will be strong within you,
and there will be no projectile barf you cannot clean.
Indeed, it might even make you taller
so you can reach those stains on the ceiling without a step ladder.

Know the personal,
yet keep to the impersonal.
Accept the World of Barf as it is.
If you accept the World of Barf,
A Man Called Da-da will be luminous inside you
and you will return to your primal self.
Well, your primal self covered in barf.
Usually in an airport.

The world is formed from the void
like utensils from a block of wood.
A Man Called Da-da knows the utensils
will be stolen by the Small Beings
and hidden amongst the Ten Thousand Things,
yet he keeps spares behind the knife block:
thus, can he cook all things...
so Small Beings can barf them up, later.

TWENTY NINE

So, Small Beings…
want to improve the world?
Try cleaning your room.
Da-da doesn't think it can be done.

The world is sacred.
It can't be improved.
Your room is a mess.
It CAN be improved.
If you tamper with the world, you'll ruin it.
If you treat it like your room, you'll lose it.
If you try to clean it,
Da-da will probably pass out from surprise.

There is a time for being behind;
a time for being in constant motion;
a time for being in constant exhaustion;
and a time for being in a dangerous frame of mind.
This is called, "Da-da Time."

A Man Called Da-da sees things as they are
without trying to control them.
Like he could.
He lets things go their own way,
and resides at the center of the mess,
in a very very messy world.

THIRTY

Whomever relies on A Man Called Da-da to govern Small Beings
doesn't try to force issues or defeat reason by force of will:
Ma-ma just hands Da-da the duct tape and heads for the hills.
For every force there is a counterforce.
For every Da-da there is a CounterDa-da
though CounterDa-da weighs more
and doesn't bathe nearly as much
(and Da-da is better looking).
And duct tape, even when well-intentioned
always sticks to itself.

Thus, A Man Called Da-da does his job
and then stops
even though *he's never really allowed to stop,*
as his job never ends, but this sounds so good to Da-da
that he had to write it.
And then Da-da stops.
But he really doesn't.
He just wanted to write it again.
See what he did there?

Da-da understands that his small redundant universe
is forever spiraling out of his control
and that trying to dominate Small Beings' events
goes against Da-da's current job profile.
Because he believes in putting himself out,
he doesn't try to convince others he's on fire.
Because he is content with himself locked in a small house,
with Small, Insane Beings who can't ever seem to stop yelling,
he doesn't need others' approval,
because no one ever comes to save him.

Because he accepts himself trapped in an endless
Parenting Mobius Loop of Horror
and Oddly Timed Satisfaction —
or writing about one —
the whole world accepts him.
Or so he tells himself.
And then it STOPS.
But it doesn't.
Damn.

THIRTY ONE

Toy lightsabers are wands of violence;
all decent Da-das detest them
when they whack Da-das in the groin.

Toy guns are the seeds of fear;
a decent Da-da will banish them
and then look the other way when they're
recreated with peaceful blocks and Legos.
If compelled, Da-da will toss them in the trash
only with the utmost restraint.
C'mon, they're expensive. Regardless,
PEACE AND QUIET are Da-da's highest values.
If the peace has been shattered,
how can Da-da be content?
(Bourbon and a little ice would help.)
No, his little monsters are not demons,
but People like himself.
They only appear to act like demons,
giggling while planting plastic explosives and fried chicken
in Da-da's underwear drawer.
He doesn't wish them personal harm.
Nor does he rejoice in victory.
How could he rejoice in victory
and delight in the incarceration
and pillorying of little monsters?
Just watch him, baby.

If pressed, Da-da enters monster battles gravely
with sorrow and great compassion,
as if he were attending his own funeral.
Da-da has to think like this.
He doesn't have much time left.

THIRTY TWO

A Man Called Da-da can't be perceived.
Sure, he's middle-aged and overweight
and has little hair or sense left,
but he's INVISIBLE to the Ten Thousand Working Things,
invisible to all save other Stay-At-Home Dads
and little monsters who can't find Baby Horsey.
Smaller than an electron,
Da-da contains uncounted universes of naked absurdity.

If powerful men — and perhaps some women —
could remain centered in their inner Da-da-ness,
all things would be in harmony.
All sippy cups would be located before they grow beards.
All Baby Horseys would boast GPS.
All playgrounds would release doves and bunnies
on the half-hour, and someone else would pick-up after them.
All Da-das would be at peace,
drinking Guinness from a refrigerated tap,
and someone else would make the beany weenies.
Of course this is all a lie.
Inner Da-da-ness is rife with denial.

When you call Da-da names,
know that they won't stick:
Da-da is Master of Selective Deafness.
When you finally put him in an institution,
just tell him it's a Three-star Resort.
Knowing when to commit Da-da
will prevent any danger.

Da-da-ness will eventually end all sanity
just as syrup flows off the table and onto the floor.

THIRTY THREE

Knowing other Da-das doesn't breed intelligence;
Da-das aren't that smart.
Knowing that Da-das are purely redundant is true wisdom;
mastering little monsters — OR MA-MA:
pure folly.
Mastering Da-da is dead-easy.
Mastering Da-da-ness is not.

When you realize you've had enough,
hunker down in the foxhole
and resolve yourself to being stinky.
At least it's quiet.
If you stay in the center
and wrap big pillows around yourself,
no thrown toy-grenade can hurt you.

THIRTY FOUR

The great Da-da-ness flows everywhere.
All things are born from it,
yet it doesn't create them.
C'mon, it's just a Y-chromosome.
It pours itself into its work,
yet makes no claim,
save for that OVUM over there.
It nourishes infinite worlds, or
it thinks it does.
Yet, it doesn't hold on to them.
Like it could.
Since it is merged with all things
and hidden in their cells,
at best, it can be called humble;
at worst, it can be called redundant.
Since all things vanish into it,
and it alone endures,
it can be called great.
It isn't aware of its greatness;
thus is it truly great.

Great.

THIRTY FIVE

Those who are centered around Da-da
feel they can go where they wish, without danger.

Those who perceive universal harmony
probably aren't paying attention.

Music, or the smell of good cooking
may make Small Beings stop and enjoy.
Or not.
Probably not.

Words that point to A Man Called Da-da
may seem monotonous and without flavor.
When you look for him, there's not much to see.
When you listen to him... what was that, again?
When you use him as a tackle dummy,
he makes satisfying OOMPH noises:
Da-da can take a lot of abuse.
But be warned:
if you abuse him too much,
he will sell all your toys on eBay.

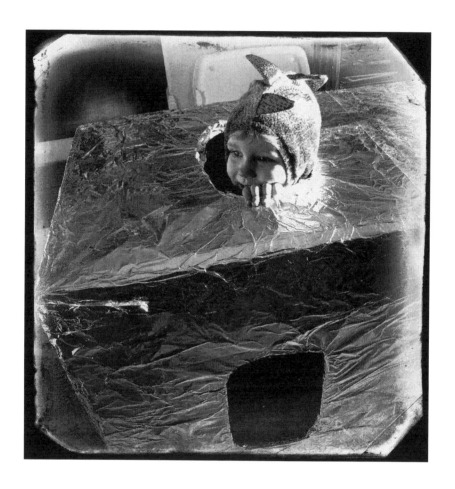

THIRTY SIX

That which shrinks
must first expand...
Da-da doesn't need to expand much more, thank you.
If you want to get rid of something,
you must first allow it to flourish...
Da-da flourished and wilted long ago.
If you want to take something,
you must first allow it to be given...
Da-da spent all his money on Legos, so do the math.
This is called the not-so-subtle perception
of the way things are.
Da-da calls it, "parenthood."

The soft overcomes the hard,
except when you run into traffic.
The slow overcomes the fast,
except when you run into traffic.
(Are you paying attention?)
Go ahead, let your ever changing kid-vectors remain a mystery.
Da-da calls this, "Evolution in Action."
If you continue to ignore the kid-safety rules,
Da-da will launch himself into orbit
where it's quiet:
in space, no one can hear you scream
at your kid.

THIRTY SEVEN

Da-da abides in non-action.
Or was that non-fiction?
Da-da abides in non-something.
Yet, nothing is left undone
but try telling that to Ma-ma.

To Ma-ma, A Man Called Da-da doesn't seem to do anything,
yet through him all things are done.
Look: the trash was taken out. SEE?

If All-powerful Ma-ma observed this,
the whole world would be transformed
and Da-da could watch the ball game in peace.
Da-da would be content
with his workaday ale,
in harmony and free of desire.
Well, mostly.

When there is a witness to suffering
and no barricades between Da-da and his ale,
all things are at peace.

THIRTY EIGHT

A Man Called Da-da doesn't try to be powerful
thus is he truly powerful.
Da-da keeps telling himself this
so HE can wear the Royal Sweatpants, if only for a little while.
The foolish Da-da reaches for power over Ma-ma;
thus is he hosed and pants-less.

A Man Called Da-da appears to do nothing
(according to Ma-ma)
yet leaves nothing undone: he rocks.
The foolish Da-da is always doing things wrong
(according to Ma-ma)
but worse, he leaves many things undone: he does not rock.

When A Man Called Da-da does something,
he leaves nothing undone. And thus, he rocks.
Please allow Da-da this small illusion.
When the foolish Da-da leaves many things to be done,
the Small Beings laugh behind his back.
If they did this to A Man Called Da-da,
the Small Beings would be wise to head for the hills.

When Da-da is lost, there is Ma-ma.
When Ma-ma is lost, there is Grandma.
When Grandma is lost, there is Grampa.
When Grampa is lost... wait, Grampa is always lost.
When grandparents are lost, there is the au pair.
When the au pair is deployed, all is lost.
The best the au pair can achieve is inane ritual.
Inane ritual is the husk of parenting without love
the beginning of chaos; be careful where you grip it.
The au pair won't grip it right,
no matter how many times you explain it,
in any language.

Therefore A Man Called Da-da concerns himself
with keeping au pairs locked in steamer trunks
for shipment back to South America or Sweden or wherever.
Da-da dwells in reality
and encourages silly debutantes who ignore his children
to propagate and talk on the phone all day elsewhere.
What choice does he have?
He has ALL the choices, baby.

THIRTY NINE

In harmony with Da-da,
the living room is clear and spacious.
Da-da's sanity is solid and full,
all Small Beings flourish together,
content with the way they are and will be,
endlessly repeating themselves and screaming;
endlessly annoying, yet in a cute way that somehow works.

When the Small Beings interfere with Da-da's writing,
the living room becomes filthy,
Da-da's sanity becomes an impossibility,
his equilibrium crumbles:
Small Beings run like hell.

A Man Called Da-da views the parts with compassion
because he understands who dug the hole.
His Y-chromosome is fraught with humility.
He doesn't glitter like a jewel.
He doesn't sing like a... a singing thing.
Instead, he lets his Royal Sweatpants be fashioned by Ma-ma,
rugged and intractable as a stone Buddha, but with boobs.
Ma-ma, not the pants.

FORTY

Gravitic collapse is the movement of Da-da.
Yielding is his way
which he learned the hard way.

All things are born of a non-local being
having a local experience.
Being is bored of non-being.
Where's the remote?

FORTY ONE

When a superior man hears of A Man Called Da-da
he immediately begins to run the other way.
When an average man hears of Da-da
he half believes it, half doubts it.
When a foolish man hears of Da-da
he laughs out loud and guns for Ma-ma
when she's fertile... and most other times, too.
If he didn't laugh,
he wouldn't become A Man Called Da-da.

Thus, it is said:
the path to Da-da-ness seems like fun;
the path forward seems like a good idea;
but the smart path usually involves some kind of birth control,
at least until you're ready to let your idea of yourself go.
Like the Ice Cream Emperor thing,
let be be finale of... something.
True power seems silly.
True purity is next to impossible — especially if
a tattoo and liquor are involved.
True steadfastness seems barely attainable
but true clarity just ain't gonna happen
until you're in the delivery room.

The greatest moment is here.
The greatest love is all over the place.
The greatest wisdom never comes to the childless.

Meanwhile, A Man Called Da-da is nowhere to be found.
He's already done all this
and is locked in the bathroom
picking Legos out of his beard.

FORTY TWO

A Man Called Da-da gives birth to no one.
He's quite happy about that.
Ma-ma on the other hand, gives birth to One.
Gives birth to Two.
Gives birth to Three.
Gives birth to all things...
and the noise is absolutely terrific.

All things have their backs to Ma-ma
and stand facing Da-da:
They have no problem with Ma-ma, you see.
If they only knew.
When Da-da and Ma-ma combine
all things achieve an NC-17-rating
that eventually — and all-too-quickly —
fall to a G-rating
at that knock on the door.

Ordinary men hate solitude
but A Man Called Da-da makes use of it,
embracing his aloneness, reflecting, realizing
wrapped in plastic
he is one with the whole universe...
if only for about ten minutes a day.

FORTY THREE

The gentlest thing in the world
overcomes the toughest thing in the world...
which explains parenthood in 13 words.
It also explains why Da-da rebounds
like a chunk of tire in Turn 3.
That which has no substance
enters where there is no space...
which explains Da-da's head in 11 words.
This shows the value of non-action.
At least Da-da thinks it does.
This also shows the potential value of
Da-da's low-cranial-pressure system.

Teaching Without Words,
Performing Without Action,
taking the Kick to the Groin
on the Couch of Destiny
while not spilling the Beer of Life:
this is Da-da's way.

FORTY FOUR

Fame or integrity
money or happiness:
which path to Ma-ma?
To be Da-da, or not to be Da-da:
that is the question.
It's a big question.

If you look to others for fulfillment
you will be a mirror with a cheap frame.
If your happiness depends on money,
you will never be happy in that convenience store job.

Be content with what you have;
rejoice in the way your clothes don't fit anymore.
When you realize there is really nothing lacking,
the whole world belongs to you.
When you realize what kid food has done to your body,
you realize how big you really are in the world.

FORTY FIVE

True perfection in the House of the Small Beings
seems impossible... because it is.
It is perfectly impossible.
True fullness in the House of the Small Beings
seems impossible... because it is.
One cannot be full unless one eats
one's damn dinner — THE DINNER ONE ASKED FOR.
Come on, Small Beings are not cats.

In the House of the Small Beings...
True action is folly;
True straightness is folly;
True wisdom is folly;
True art is folly, but with a pricetag.

A Man Called Da-da allows these things to happen
because he is lame.
He is like a reed in a supernova:
his life bends, burns and is totally obliterated
in a blink of reverse birth-control.
The rest is non-silence.
Meanwhile, Da-da dodges events as they come,
steps out of the way,
and lets The Tao of Da-da speak for itself.

FORTY SIX

When the Lawn Gorillas... er, Small Beings are
in harmony with A Man Called Da-da
his factories make cupcakes and sugar cookies.
When the Small Beings go counter to Da-da:
broccoli-bran muffins are stacked by the gate.

There is no greater motivator than a scary muffin,
no greater wrong than serving one to make a point,
no greater misfortune than having to eat one yourself.

Whomever can see through fearful muffins
and find the inner frosted cupcake,
will always be safe.

FORTY SEVEN

Without opening your door
you can open your heart to the world...
and make a really big mess in the living room.
Without looking out your window
you can see the essence of Da-da...
yeah, there's a unicorn in there
but it's a MEAN unicorn.

As usual, the more you know
the less you understand.

A Man Called Da-da leaves without arriving,
is blind without looking,
and does everything,
while achieving nothing:
it's a living.

FORTY EIGHT

In the pursuit of knowledge
every day is something added.
In the practice of being A Man Called Da-da
every day some brain cell goes missing.
Or sometimes a whole brain.

Less and less does one need to force things;
inertia can do that to a person.
Indeed, when nothing is done
nothing is left undone
until one's feet find Legos
one time too many.
On the stairs.
In the middle of the night.

True mastery over the small and the plastic
can be gained by letting
Lego starship trajectories go their own way,
touch-up paint being the better part of valor.

FORTY NINE

A Man Called Da-da has no mind of his own.
His children ate it.

Still, he is good to people who are good.
He is good to people who are not good.
Da-da is a sap.

He trusts people who are trustworthy.
He trusts people who are not exactly trustworthy, but
play one on TV.
Da-da enjoys abuse.

A Man Called Da-da's mind is like space
but with better planets.
That serve coffee 24/7.
People don't understand him.
How could they?
They look at him and shake their heads.
Some throw rocks.
He treats them like his own children
with a voice like a Fallen Angel.

FIFTY

A Man Called Da-da tries to yield
to whatever the moment brings... er, demands.
He knows his head is filled mostly with air.
No illusions remain in his indentured worldview.
No resistance in his will.
His mind and will are gone, like the government,
lost in a pile of robots and sharp plastic things.
Da-da doesn't think about things anymore,
about his endless repetitive actions,
because there's rarely time for that.
Da-da's actions flow from the Core of Whatever
to carve out the Valley of Ok, Da-da.
Da-da holds nothing back from life
because Da-da signed up for this.
The flow is the go
and strong winds CAN blow all day,
depending on how much sugar has been ingested.
Da-da knows when he's beat.
He folds and patiently awaits a new deal,
a Brave Frontier at summer's end:
The hope, the promise
of Back-to-School.

FIFTY ONE

Small Beings in the House
are not exactly expressions of A Man Called Da-da
any more than a hand is a handful.
They spring into every day
nearly unconscious,
wholly perfect and free and quasi-undisciplined
and, of course, loud as hell.
Perfect spirit, they appear to take on a physical body —
if that body can keep up —
and bounce that somatic, rubbery bag of glop off walls and cats
and furniture,
letting circumstance be their insane riding chicken.
That's why every Small Being in the house
spontaneously ignores A Man Called Da-da:
they can't hear him over Ma-ma's screaming.

Sure, A Man Called Da-da gives birth to all Housemade People
in a feckless Y-chromosome kinda way;
he nourishes them, maintains them,
hoses them down, puts out their fires,
totes around the unwieldy Pillar of Common Sense
for them to goggle at incomprehendingly,
and looks the other way when they knock it over.
He takes them back to himself as often as he can,
creating without creativity,
acting without acting experience,
guiding without a goddamn clue.
That's why love of A Man Called Da-da
is an impossible thing not to do:
everyone loves an Underdog.

FIFTY TWO

In the beginning was A Man Called Da-da.
Nothing much came of him.
Not much returned to him.

In the beginning was Ma-ma.
All things issued from her.
All things returned to her.

To find your source
trace back the manifestations.
When you recognize your children
under all that dirt
and finally find Ma-ma,
you will be free of sorrow
because *she now has the kid duty*:
tag, you're it.

If you close your mind in old male-female roles
and get caught in desire-traffic,
your heart will boom for Vegas.
If you keep your mind open,
and keep your senses in the driveway,
your heart will find peace.
(Be sure to start it once a month.)

Seeing into darkness is clarity
but only when children are screaming.
Knowing how to win by losing
is pretty much all you've got.
Use your headlights
and look down the road for obstructions.
This is called defensive parenting.

FIFTY THREE

The Tao of Da-da, the Great Way is easy,
its guard rails supreme and unblemished.
Yet, people prefer crooked, rocky side roads.
Beware the unpaved frontage roads
filled with attorneys and no patience.
Stay on the High Way (not that high, Maurice)
with A Man Called Da-da, in the middle lane,
in his SuperCamper Special.
He may not have all the answers,
but he knows the locations of all the best taco stands.

When the wealthy prosper
while farmers lose their land;
when the government wastes money
on weaponry instead of food and medicine;
when the upper class drives Lambourghinis and Ferarris
while the poor sit on the side of the road...
all this is robbery and chaos
and pretty much business as usual on Planet Earth.
It is not in keeping with A Man Called Da-da.
Da-da will always let you drive his SuperCamper Special
provided you help with gas
(c'mon, it gets 12 mpg).
Drive on and watch for taco stands.

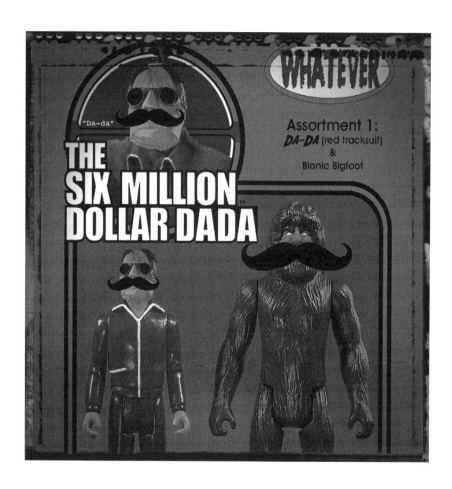

FIFTY FOUR

Whoever is planted with A Man Called Da-da
will not be rooted up.
Whoever embraces A Man Called Da-da
will not slip away.
Your name will be held in honor
from generation to generation...
ok, who's Da-da kidding?
People don't even know his real name.

Let A Man Called Da-da be present in your life
and you will become genuine.
Well, kinda.
Let him be present in your family
and WATCH as the coffee and danishes VANISH.
Let him be present in your country
and your country will be an example
to all countries in the world
of how to embrace A Man Caled Da-da
as a great artist and local tax-free celebrity.
Let him be present in the universe
and... well, sure, the universe will sing,
but the hat will be a little less full
of itself.

How does Da-da know this to be true?
Da-da is OLD.
He's been looking inside himself so long
he's starting to see things.

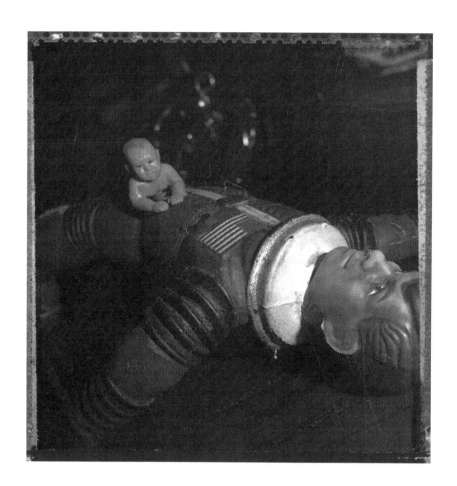

FIFTY FIVE

He who is in harmony with A Man Called Da-da
is like a newborn baby
naked and defenseless.
Sure, his bones are soft, his muscles weak
but his grip on your short hairs is unbelievable;
the child doesn't know about the previous union
of male and female
'cause we kept the door locked, c'mon.
Yet, that grip is always there, even through the closed door.
Ow.
So intense is his vital power
that our little Lord Fauntleroy can scream all day
yet never become hoarse...
until the doctor asks why his voice sounds like that.
So complete is little King Nebuchaddnezzer's harmony
because the little bastard knows who's really in control.

A Man Called Da-da's power is kinda like that.
Kinda.
He lets things come and go,
talking of Michelangelo,
without the desire of becoming
a teenage mutant ninja turtle himself.
Like them, he rarely expects results.
Why should he start now?
Da-da's low expectations mean
Da-da's never disappointed,
thus does his spirit never grow any older
than the dirt on the ground
that will be covering him up shortly.

FIFTY SIX

Those who don't have Small Beings don't listen
to those who do,
because they know everything.
If those who don't have Small Beings listened
to those who do,
the human race would die out pretty damn quick.

As a parent, you close your mouth. Why?
It won't do any good.
Your senses are blocked off due to too much screaming.
Your sharpness is blunted due to no sleep.
Your knots are all untied by little hands.
Your knots are all tied by little hands.
Your glare is softened by sleep in your eyes.
Your house is dust-free due to constant running.
Your uncarved block has been completely CARVED
thankyouverymuch.
This is known as being DONE as a parent.

Being done is inevitable; your primal identity.
If you tell non-parents about it,
the human race will grind to a halt
and everyone will head for the pits —
or floor it and smash into the wall at Turn Three.
There's no straightaway in the human race.

Instead, be like A Man Called Da-da.
He can't be approached or withdrawn from,
benefited or harmed,
honored or brought into disgrace...
because Da-da continually gives up,
waving a white flag from the Couch of Forgetfulness.
Like the Dude, the Da-da abides.

FIFTY SEVEN

If you want to be a great leader
you must learn to follow A Man Called Da-da.
Or ignore him completely,
one or the other.
Either way, stop trying to control.
Parenting isn't about control.
Parenting is about acceptance, duty
and the cleaning of debris.

Let go of fixed plans and concepts
and the world will govern itself.
Or totally fall apart.
It looks the same either way.

Therefore, A Man Called Da-da says:
Let go of the rules
and let the principal do his/her job;
Let go of economics
and watch the prosperous get all the good Legos;
Let go of religion
'cause Small Beings will never be quiet when necessary;
Let go of desire for the common good
and pray for the uncommon good to land on your lawn.

When in doubt, make a public call to Santa:
Santa is the only Law to Small Beings.

FIFTY EIGHT

When things are governed by Pokemon,
the Small Beings are simple and honest.
When things are governed by Team Rocket,
the Small Beings are depressed and sneaky.

Misfortune thy name is parenthood.
It's what fortune depends upon
'cause without duality there's only one thing:
A Man Called Da-da.
Fortune is where misfortune hides its dirty socks.
Who knows their ultimate end?
Da-da does: behind the dryer.
This is their predetermined outcome
as only ONE sock can prevail —
ONE SOCK TO RULE THEM ALL —
and it usually has holes in it.
The missing right sock checks to its sinister.
Goodness lasts only as long as the fabric softener holds out.
The confusion of whose sock is whose
lasts many long days until one realizes
that it's time to buy more socks
and you'd better keep track of them this time, Timmy.

Thus is A Man Called Da-da
righteous without being right,
incorruptible but relatively extravagant when it comes to socks,
straightforward with the use of the spin cycle,
and illuminated enough to know
when things are dry enough.
The buzzer helps.

FIFTY NINE

For governing a family well,
there is nothing better than moderating in moderation.
The mark of a moderate Da-da
is family freedom from Da-da's own ideas;
these usually conflict with Ma-ma's ideas, so why have them?
Tolerant as a Vegas waitress,
pervasive as cracks in Da-da's driveway,
firm like a chicken,
supple like another chicken,
Da-da himself has no destination in view,
'cause he's not going anywhere fast.
Da-da makes use of whatever
life happens to bring his way,
and keeps duct tape close at hand.
Nothing is impossible for his mind,
except for the fact that he just made that up.

SIXTY

Governing a household full of Small Beings —
or any beings for that matter —
is like hitting yourself in the head repeatedly
with a ball peen hammer:
it feels so good when you stop.

Center your attention on A Man Called Da-da
and evil will have no power.
Not that it isn't out there,
it's just never at the meetings.
You'll be able to easily step out of its way
when it guns its motor,
'cause its clutch slips something awful.
Give evil a moving target
and it will usually miss.
Usually.

SIXTY ONE

When a Da-da basks in infrequent, transient praise,
he becomes like a Christmas tree:
he'll have to come down eventually.
The brighter he grows,
the greater the need to replace his bulbs.
Replacing lots of bulbs means trusting A Man Called Da-da.
Or just finding a used Da-da on eBay.

A great Mr. Mom...er, Da-da, is like a great man;
he's not a great man, just LIKE one.
When A Man Called Da-da makes a mistake
he doesn't have to realize it: it's realized for him.
Having realized it, he lives it.
Having lived it, he stares at it in the mirror for hours.
He considers those who point out his faults as redundant.
And he thinks of his enemy
as the shadow that he himself casts,
as it seems to keep getting bigger.

If a nation is centered on A Man Called Da-da,
Da-da will know he's dreaming.
If it nourishes its own people,
Hell will freeze over... kinda like it's doing now.
And if said nation doesn't meddle in the affairs of others...
like Da-da, no one will believe it.
It will be a light to all nations in the world on what not to do,
making that bulb-replacement thing all the more important.

SIXTY TWO

A Man Called Da-da is the center of the universe.
(He is, too.)
He's a good woman's treasure
and a bad man-refuge.
Not exactly sure what that means in the long-run.

Honors can be bought with fine words.
Respect can be won with good deeds.
But A Man Called Da-da is beyond all value
and no one believes it.

Thus, when a new Da-da comes along,
don't offer to help him
with your wealth or your expertise.
Offer instead
to teach him about A Man Called Da-da
so he can know what not to do
and perhaps even run like hell while he still can.
Or learn how to do the job and THRIVE
for a few days before they have to bury him.

Why do the Ancient Da-da Masters esteem
A Man Called Da-da?
They don't: they pity him.
Being one with Da-da,
you find your head in your hands.
You also find that it is either empty
or clogged with Legos.
And when you make a mistake,
you'll know you really are like Da-da.
That is why everyone wonders about the Y-chromosome.

SIXTY THREE

Act without doing.
Work without effort.
Vacuum as little as possible.
Think of the small as large
and the few as many,
regardless of how many Legos you step on.
Confront the difficult
while it is still easy,
'cause it never is.
Accomplish the great task
by a series of small acts
of madness.

A Man Called Da-da never reaches for the great,
thus he achieves greatness.
He keeps telling himself this.
When he runs into difficulty,
he stops and gives himself to it;
he doesn't cling to his own comfort
as that's clearly beyond his job description.
Thus are problems no problem for him
because their solution is no solution at all.
Ambiguity is Da-da's magic flying carpet.
Evil, thy name is Lego.

SIXTY FOUR

What is rooted is getting into your pipes.
What is recent is largely forgotten.
What is brittle broke a long time ago.
What is small has probably been eaten by the cat.

Prevent trouble before it arises.
Go ahead, try!
Put things in order before they exist...
just don't expect it to work.
The giant pine tree grows from a tiny nut
eaten by a rodent and pooped somewhere.
The journey of a thousand miles
starts when parents wake up in the morning.

Rushing to action, you fail —
usually because of toys on the stairs. Or cats.
Trying to grasp things, tails, you lose them:
you can only carry so much.
Forcing a homework project to completion
is only possible by threatening to call Santa.

Therefore A Man Called Da-da takes action
by letting things take their course into oblivion.
He remains as calm at the end as at the beginning
or perhaps insensate is a better word
since Da-da has already reached The End.
He has nothing,
absolutely nothing,
thus has nothing to lose.

What he desires is non-desire
mostly because he's stuck with it.
He not so much learns to unlearn
as he does forget to learn how to remember.
He simply reminds people
of who they have always been
by his obsequious example.
He cares nothing about A Man Called Da-da
because he's caring for all things
that are clogging the toilet again.

SIXTY FIVE

The Ancient Da-da Masters
didn't try to educate the Small Beings;
instead, they kindly taught them
not to inform on the Ancient Da-da Masters
in exchange for things the Ancient Ma-ma Masters
had already said, "NO" to.

When Small Beings take advantage of this —
and suppose that they themselves know all the answers —
they are difficult to guide,
mostly because you don't want to guide them
so much as let them fall on their faces...
which is technically a form of guidance.
When Small Beings find they know that they DON'T know,
they're usually parents themselves,
and the curse has worked yet again.

If you want to learn how to govern,
avoid being clever or rich,
but seriously invest in birth control.
The simplest pattern is the clearest:
the rhythm method MAKES PARENTS.
Eventually accepting what you intentionally did to your life
you begin to show all childless people the way
toward being parents themselves,
so the curse lives on forever.

SIXTY SIX

All streams flow to the sea
by way of the stairs,
because the sea is lower than the stairs, HELLO?
Humility gives it its power.
Or robs it.
One of those.

If you want to govern Small Beings,
you must place yourself below them,
while at the same time
expecting a full body slam,
or head-butt to the groin.
If you want to lead Small Beings,
you must learn how to endure abuse.

A Man Called Da-da is above Small Beings,
because they tied him.
He goes ahead of the Small Beings,
because heavy things fall faster downhill.
The whole world is grateful to him
because he has The Duty,
freeing others to VIVE MUCHACHA.

Because Da-da competes with no one
no one can compete with him…
which sounds noble, but it's actually a prelude
to a kind of being-and-nothingness simultaneity
which no one understands until
they fall into the parent trap
where CUTENESS grabs you for just an instant…
and you're a goner.
If it weren't for cuteness, the human race
would've vanished millions of years ago.

SIXTY SEVEN

Some say that Da-da's teaching is nonsense
and nonsensical.
Others call it lofty and impractical.
But to those who have looked inside themselves
and found that gooey center,
this nonsense makes perfect sense... nonsensically.
And to those who put it into practice
any loftiness is laughable.

Da-da has just three things to teach — no, **FOUR**:
simplicity and patience, compassion and humor.
These are your greatest treasures.
Simple in action and in thought,
you return to the source of being clueless
mostly via kid-induced brain damage.
Patient with both friends and enemies,
you are **ONE** with the way things are
because you've been cleaning up **TWO** all day.
Compassionate toward yourself,
you reconcile all People, so long as
they stop screaming and do what you ask them to do
the first time you ask them to do it.
Thus are you rarely compassionate toward yourself
or anyone who looks like you,
and laughter comes when you try to speak,
or make any kind of sense in public.
But Da-da knows a secret:
What is it that transcends Small Beings and Matriarchs alike?
Cupcake!

SIXTY EIGHT

The best athlete
sometimes wants his opponent tired and downtrodden.
The best general
often destroys the mind of his enemy.
The best businessman
serves himself, but good.
The best leader...
well, we stopped having those.

All of these embody
the "virtue" of competition.
Not that they don't love to compete against those worthy
like any Capitalist, they just want to win at all costs.
In this they are like Da-da's children
and badly in need of a time-out
in the mirror room.

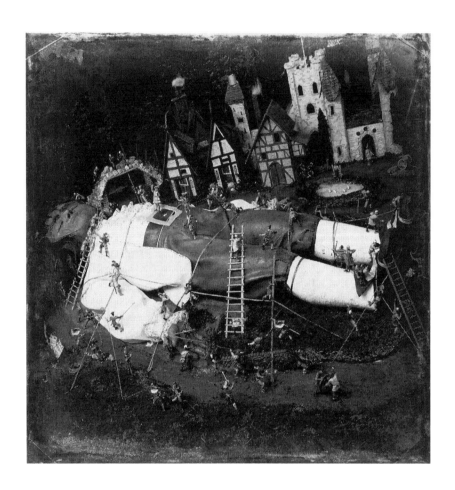

SIXTY NINE

The Ancient Da-da Masters have a saying:
"Rather than make the first move
it is better to wait and see what the in-laws have planned.
Be prepared to retreat a mile — give or take a thousand."

This is called:
"Going forward without advancing
pushing back without getting caught."
This is also called, "dealing with family."

There is no greater misfortune
than underestimating the horrors of your extended family.
It's not that they're evil
just self-absorbed to the point of physical combustion.

Remember:
when two great forces oppose each other
the victory will go
to the one who knows how to win by losing.
A good supply of bourbon helps, too.

SEVENTY

A Man Called Da-da's teachings are easy to understand
and easy to put into practice
provided you've checked your Yang at the door.
("Excuse me. Is this your Yang?")
Your intellect may balk at this,
but what's it done for you lately?

Da-da's teachings are older than the world.
Or maybe it's Da-da that's older than the world.
How can you grasp Da-da's meaning?
If you want to know Da-da,
review the Ten-fold Path of the 10,000 Things:

>   1. Have children
>   2. Change 10,000 diapers
>   3. Catch barf 10,000 times (one feels like a thousand)
>   4. Plan and make 10,000 meals
>   5. Worry 10,000 x 10,000 times
>   6. Enter into the Santa Conspiracy (about 10,000 days)
>   7. Sleep — fully — once every 10,000 hours
>   8. Bathe — fully — once every 10,000 hours
>   9. Lose 10,000 x 10,000 x 10,000 x 10,000 x 10,000 neurons
>   10. Number things without mercy, or regret.

Another way to know Da-da (non-biblically) is to simply
look for the grizzled guy with the grizzled beard.
See him staring into space?
Why does he stare into space?
That's where he lives.
Who is he?
Chances are that's Da-da.
Or a mental patient.
Or both.

SEVENTY ONE

Not-knowing is true knowledge.
Thus, Da-da is a genius.
Presuming to know is a disease.
Thus, Da-da is supremely healthy.
First realize you want to be a parent,
then check yourself into a mental hospital.

A Man Called Da-da is his own physician
primarily because all the other ones want to lock him up.
He has healed himself of all knowing...
which is a fancy way of saying his mind is gone.
Thus, Da-da is truly whole and built to endure,
so long as he stays in his hole.

SEVENTY TWO

When Small Beings lose their sense of awe,
they turn to glowing screens.
When they no longer trust A Man Called Da-da,
they become an authority.

Therefore the Da-da Master steps back
so people won't be confused about
who's holding the door open.
Da-da teaches without teaching,
because no one would believe him otherwise.

SEVENTY THREE

A Man Called Da-da is always at ease.
Or perhaps that's just catatonia.
He overcomes without competing
because he wins by losing
and answers without speaking a word;
no one can understand him anyway.
He arrives without being summoned
because he never left the house.
He is his own boss
but not really.

His net covers the Whole Universe of Acquiescence.
And though his meshes are wide and fraying,
he doesn't let a thing slip through so much as he lets
everything fall through *him*
and all over the floor.

A man without a plan is a canal.
Therefore, A Man Called Da-da is in Panama.

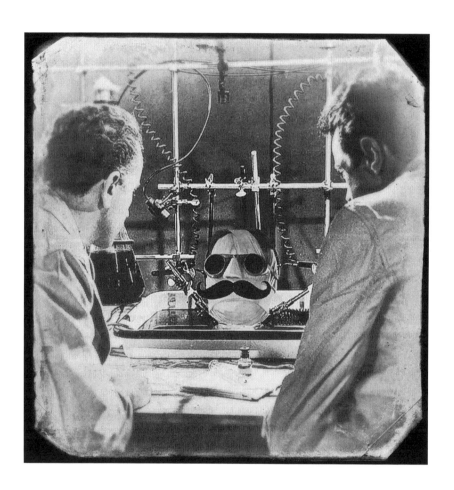

SEVENTY FOUR

If you realize that all things change,
there is nothing you need to hold on to.
When you realize that all things Small Being
WILL NEED TO BE CHANGED,
there is no diaper you won't try.
If you aren't afraid of dying,
there is nothing you can't achieve.
If you aren't afraid of parenthood,
there's something wrong with you.
Unless you're a wonder.
One of those.

Trying to control the future
is like eating a chainsaw:
you generally fall to pieces
but you can still live
after a fashion.

SEVENTY FIVE

When expectations are too high,
Small Beings go crazy.
When A Man Called Da-da is too intrusive,
Small Beings plot the Nerf Coup.

Act for the Small Beings' benefit.
Appear to trust them
without trusting them one bit.
Leave them alone,
while spying on them around the corner.

SEVENTY SIX

Women are born soft and supple;
after they reproduce, they oftimes become stiff and hard
mostly when you fail to do what they ask you to do
the first time they ask you to do it.
Plants are born tender and pliant;
after they reproduce, they are oftimes brittle and dry
with sharp nasty thorns
and a propensity for disrespecting Da-da.

Thus, whoever is stiff and inflexible
is a disciple of pain,
because they hurt when they hit.
Whoever is soft and yielding
is a disciple of life,
or a spastic nerfbag like Da-da.

Ah, but the hard and stiff will be broken.
The soft and supple and spastically nerfbaggy will prevail.
Failing that, we sleep
on the Couch of Triumph in the
Family Room of Obliscence.

SEVENTY SEVEN

As he acts in the world, A Man Called Da-da
is like the bending of a bow:
his top is bent downward,
his bottom is bent up,
his middle breaks accordingly.
Da-da adjusts excess and deficiency
so there is perfect balance...
ok, a little weighted toward deficiency, let's not fool ourselves.
He may take from what is too much
and give to what isn't enough,
but everyone's gonna bitch that someone else got more.

Those who try to control
and use force to protect their perceived power,
go against A Man Called Da-da *AND* his surly unicorn.
Those who take from those who don't have
and give to those who have too much
are SO going to bed early without TV or dessert.

A Man Called Da-da can keep giving
because there is no end to his wealth.
There's no beginning, either.
Welcome to the Da-da Paradox.
Da-da acts without expectation,
succeeds without actually succeeding,
and doesn't think he's better than anyone else, 'cause...
he's A Man Called Da-da.
Da-da has been sitting at the back of the bus —
and sometimes under the bus —
but for only a decade, or two.

SEVENTY EIGHT

Nothing in the world
is as soft and yielding as water –
except maybe Da-da
but you would expect that.
Yet, for dissolving the hard and inflexible,
nothing can surpass Da-da coffee.

The Nerf overcomes the rock.
The white Santa beard overcomes the clean-shaven.
Everyone knows this is true.
But few can put it into practice
because most are still scratching their heads.

Therefore, A Man Called Da-da remains
a serene example in the midst of sorrow,
serenity being the teflon of life.
Sorrow and evil cannot enter Da-da's heart
because it's already had so many holes poked in it;
evil and sorrow just fall on the floor and can't get up.
Since Da-da has given up helping negativity get up off the floor,
Da-da is a Small Being's greatest help.

True words seem paradoxical, and…
well, a little funny.
And, well… monstrous.

SEVENTY NINE

Failure is an opportunity.
If you blame someone else
there's no end to blaming yourself,
unless you're sure you can get away with it.

Therefore, A Man Called Da-da
uses the word, "therefore" a lot,
fulfilling his own obligations
and correcting his own mistakes,
while running away at top speed.
He does what he needs to do
and demands little of others.
They aren't going to do what he asks, anyway.

EIGHTY

If a household is governed wisely
its inhabitants will be content
so long as they take undue credit for it.
They enjoy the labor of others' hands
and don't waste time inventing labor-saving machines:
that's why they have Da-da.
Since they dearly love their home
Small Beings aren't interested in travel
unless there's a stuffed animal in it for them.

There may be a few wagons and boats strewn all over the yard
but these don't go anywhere unless Da-da pulls them.
There may be an arsenal of soft weapons
but no one can find any Nerf ammunition.
(Psst, the cat chews 'em up.)
Small Beings enjoy their food
(if it's got enough chocolate sauce on it);
take pleasure in being with their family
(if there's something in it for them);
spend weekends working in the garden
(if they're paid lavishly);
and delight in the doings of the neighborhood
(watching to see if the boobytraps worked).

And even though the next household over is close enough
that the Small Beings can hear other Small Beings
crowing and barking and screaming, each
is content to WHOOP their own little WHOOP of triumph
'cause they will inherit the earth,
if they can ever get those bags off their heads.

EIGHTY ONE

True words aren't eloquent
but they are rather pokey
when you try them on.
Eloquent words aren't true —
except these.
Wise men don't need to prove their point
mostly because people generally ignore them.
Men who need to prove their point
aren't A Man Called Da-da:
Da-da *is* pointless.
But he does have a point.

A Man Called Da-da has no possessions.
That would require money. And time.
The more Da-da does for others,
the happier they are.
The more he gives to others,
the wealthier they are.
Who's idea was this, anyway?

A Man Called Da-da nourishes by not forcing —
he's not making *fois gras*, here.
By not dominating, A Man Called Da-da
leads the way
to the back of the bus,
already in progress.
Tickets, please.

EIGHTY TWO

They say it's always darkest before
the dawn, but it's really quite bright
with the right light.

Just as an acorn
is a program
for an oak;

Just as Congress
is a play
we all pay not to see;

Just as the ME decade
fell unceremoniously
into the WHY ME decade;

And just as Da-da's offspring
continue to confuse cotton candy with
haunted candy;

So goes the learned man,
the learned plan,
the learned canal.

Da-da thinks
therefore he is
Rene Descartes.

ADDENDUM: *MISC. DA-DA*

Contents

Da-da's Rules of Pillow-Fight Club	p181
Da-da's Rules of Food Club	p183
The Da-da Trench Test	p185
This is My Diaper	p191
Da-da's New & Improved Human Classifications for a Better Tomorrow	p193

THE *OTHER* ADDENDUM

Contents

All the Pretty Postmodern Carols	pp197-261
Other Stuff	pp263-267

ADDENDUM #1
DA-DA'S RULES OF PILLOW-FIGHT CLUB

1st RULE: You do not talk about PILLOW FIGHT CLUB (esp. to Ma-ma).

2nd RULE: You DO NOT TALK about PILLOW FIGHT CLUB (Jeez, why would you want to?).

3rd RULE: If someone says "stop," their pillow goes limp, or taps out, the pillow fight is over.

4th RULE: Only two pillows to a fight. Or maybe four. But no more than eight.

5th RULE: One pillow fight at a time. Unless someone yells, "PILLOW CARNAGE!"

6th RULE: Eye protection. Wear it.

7th RULE: Pillow fights will go on *as long as they have to*.

8th RULE: If this is your first night at PILLOW FIGHT CLUB, you HAVE to fight.

9th RULE: Bring your own pillow.

10th RULE: No cheap shots at Da-da.

ADDENDUM #2
DA-DA'S RULES OF FOOD CLUB

1st RULE: You do not scream during FOOD CLUB.

2nd RULE: You DO NOT scream during FOOD CLUB. (Except when you're screaming.)

3rd RULE: If someone says "bug!" or their fork sticks in the wall, the meal is over.

4th RULE: Only two plates to a diner. Or maybe four. But no more than eight.

5th RULE: One meal at a time. Unless the in-laws are here.

6th RULE: Eye protection. Wear it.

7th RULE: Meals will go on as long as they have to.

8th RULE: If you requested a specific food for FOOD CLUB, you HAVE to eat.

9th RULE: Eat your own food.

10th RULE: Slow down and chew your food like a reasonably sane rabid animal.

11th RULE: If you're gonna eat, your mouth will be involved.

12th RULE: No food fights – or YOU clean it up.

13th RULE: Grooving while you eat is allowed, but only for really good egg salad.

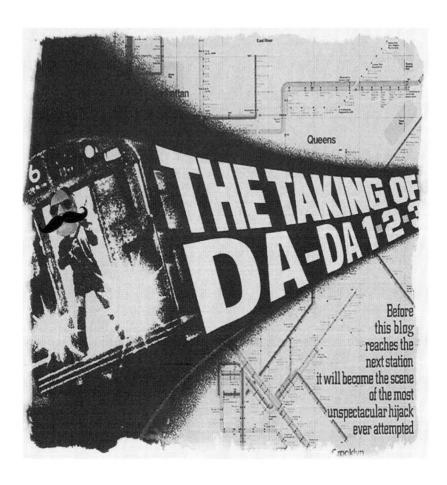

ADDENDUM #3
THE DA-DA TRENCH TEST

Answer YES to more than ten of the below questions,
CONGRATULATIONS: *you're a parent. Or perhaps a teenager.*

1. Do you feel exhausted from little or no sleep/being up all night, your fatigue the stuff of legend?

2. Are you perpetually rumpled, dirty, unclean, unshaven, unkempt, perhaps even STINKY – in public – and find that you simply don't care?

3. Have you started to resemble Chewbacca? Make Wookie noises?

4. Do you often find yourself wearing the same clothes over and over, day after day?

5. Do you find yourself scarfing cold greasy food while standing up/walking/running?

6. Have you found that you not only LIKE beany weenies, but talk about them in public?

7. Do you occasionally find yourself screaming?

8. Do you occasionally find yourself screaming the same thing over and over?

9. Do you often scream or pontificate about beany weenies?

10. Has your memory... um, is the... what was the question?

11. Do the strangest things often come flying in from every direction? Or out of your mouth?

12. Have the terms, "debris field" and "unholy terror," become relative?

13. Do you find yourself schlepping heavy, screaming things over great distances in a kind of endless death march?

14. Do you go to the bathroom as quickly as possible while someone outside is screaming and pounding on the door?

15. Do you bark orders at troops who are selectively deaf and most probably brain-damaged?

16. Have you become jaded to crying and shouting and fighting? To other people's crying and shouting and fighting?

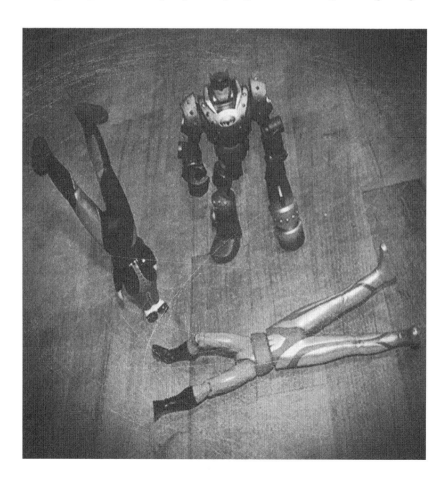

17. Is one of your eyes now bigger than the other? Is it twitching?

18. Have you ever accidently started making breakfast for dinner, then just gone with it?

19. Are you often strapping people into things and checking the straps, repeatedly?

20. Have you seriously considered using duct tape as an enforcer?

21. On rare breaks, do you stare into space, numb and insensate? (AKA, the Thousand-yard Stare.)

22. Have you, for all intents and purposes, become celebate for long periods? Forever?

23. Do you wish you'd always been celebate, living alone on some mountain with wolves?

24. Have you started to look like two wolves in one set of clothes?

25. Have you read part of a parenting book, tossed it aside and muttered: "Yeah, right"?

26. Have you stepped on mines (toys) barefoot, and silently screamed/cursed in pain?

27. When running errands at lightspeed, have you found you instinctively KNOW what every crying baby/toddler/kid wants, even when it's not your kid?

28. Have you, the parenting veteran, muttered the answer to the clueless newbie parents of the child? (e.g., "He's HUNGRY, you idiot.")

29. Do you live in fear of strollers?

30. Do you now take even the most unspeakable of bodily acts at face-value?

31. Have you come in contact with blood, vomit, feces, urine, hair, smooshed/uneaten food all in the same hour? In the same minute?

32. Have you ever caught barf? Someone else's barf?

33. Do 90% of your sentences begin with, "Awright, you monkeys...."

34. Have you ever threatened to call Santa? The Easter Bunny? The Tooth Fairy? The FBI Crime Lab? All four? At the same time?

35. Have you, or your commander, simultaneously giggled and cried while making your 19th cup of coffee with shaking hands?

36. Have you fallen to calling your commander "mommy"?

37. Do you ever find yourself replacing curse words with nonsense words that sound the same? (e.g., "BOB SAGET!!")

38. Do you find yourself angrily sputtering the wrong name, mixing up the names of your kids with the names of your cat or dog or spouse? Bob Saget?

39. Do you leer at happy childless couples and jealously conjure lurid Hammer Film/Dracula moments?

40. Have you begun to notice a resemblance between yourself and Christopher Lee as Dracula? Oliver Reed as the Werewolf? Martha Stewart?

41. Do Grimm's Fairy Tales make you laugh out loud?

42. Is Dr. Suess starting to make sense?

43. Have you ever hidden *Goodnight Moon* in the freezer?

44. Do you often feel you'd be happier blown to bits by a 110 mm shell? A 220 mm shell? 440?

45. Have you learned to despise anyone who not only makes long-ass parenting lists, but who also can't seem to express themselves in less than 140 characters?

ADDENDUM #4
THIS IS MY DIAPER

To be memorized/chanted by Small Beings, a la "Full Metal Jacket."

"This is my diaper. There are many like it but this one is mine. My diaper is my best friend. It is my life. I must master it as I must master my life. Without me, my diaper is useless. Without my diaper, I am useless. I must use my diaper true. I must poop straighter than my brother, who is trying to pull my diaper off. I must poop before he does. I will. I must not poop in my pants. Ever. Before Da-da I swear this creed: my diaper and myself are defenders of my pants, we are the masters of poop, we are the saviors of my pants. So be it, until there are no pants, but peace. Amen."

ADDENDUM #5
DA-DA's New & Improved
HUMAN GROUP CLASSIFICATIONS
For a Better Tomorrow

Family

A GAZE of moms
A RESIGNATION of Dads
A HIDING of Stay-At-Home Dads (SAHDs)
A MUDDLE of uncles
An EMPIRE of aunts
A SHREWDNESS of grandmas
A PUTTERING of grampas
A CONFUSION of cousins
A SCURRY of children
A DESTRUCTION of teens
A SLOTH of au pairs
An INSISTENCE of biological clocks
A BUMP of preggers

School

A PANDEMONIUM of preschoolers
A COLLISION of kindergarteners
A MULLING of 1st graders
A LAUNCH of 2nd graders
A SKIP of 3rd graders
A TRUDGE of 4th graders
A BRACE of 5th graders
A CHARM of 6th graders
A BROOD of 7th graders
A CONFUSION of 8th graders
A GULP of freshmen

A BASH of sophomores
A CARLOAD of juniors
An OMNISCIENCE of seniors
An INTRIGUE of princesses
An INFECTION of BigMenOnCampus
A TASK of teachers
A QUIVER of substitute teachers
A POMP of principals
A CIRCUMCISION of administrators
A PRIDE of professors
A SMACK of fraternities
A SCOURGE of sororities
An ENTITLEMENT of millenials

The Modern World

A SEIGE of chores
An INFINITY of grocery lists
A SMIRK of executives (w/jobs)
A SHUFFLE of executives (w/o jobs)
A WAKE of Starbuckminsters
A HISS of baristas
An INVOCATION of attorneys
A BLOAT of banksters
An UNKINDNESS of CEOs
A SMACK of boardroom amazons
A NUISANCE of marketers
A BUSINESS of assistants
A SNIDE of specialists
A TEDIUM of transportation officials
A VIOLATION of border officials
An INTRUSION of media
A COLLISION of insurance salesmen
A FLAMBOYANCE of hairdressers
An IMPLAUSIBILITY of da-da-ists
An INFESTATION of politicians
A SNOOP of intelligence agents/agencies
A SLEUTH of detectives

A SILLINESS of celebrities
A STUBBORNNESS of spouses
A WRECK of artists
A MUTATION of cosplayers
A PLAGUE of hipsters
A FEVER of writers [unpublished]
A DESCENT of authors [published]
A SNIP of editors
An IMPOSSIBILITY of publishers
A ROWLING of Hogwartsians
A NUISANCE of muggles
A DEFENESTRATION of Da-da's
A JUDGEMENT of lists

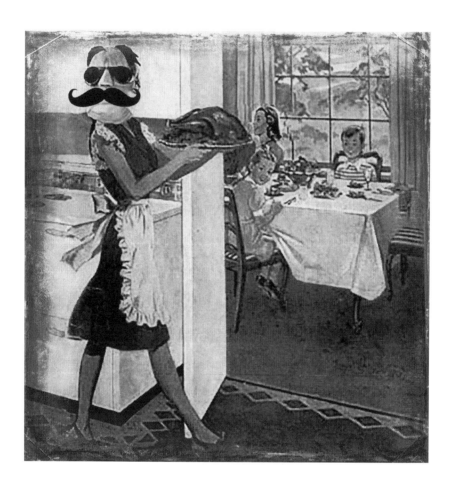

THE *OTHER* ADDENDUM

ALL THE PRETTY POSTMODERN CAROLS

Da-da used to be a musician. He is in fact a recovering musician, which means he still has *some* vestigial musicality left (psst, he doesn't really) in what's left of his mind, and occasionally a tune will get in there and rattle around until he makes fun of it, in which case it gets offended and goes away. This seems to often occur during menial parenting tasks.

The following pages are examples of those moments where Da-da had something happen to him and a "WHAMMY" (aka, "earworm") got stuck in Da-da's head until his head exploded, or he started speaking in Furbish (AGAIN). Da-da calls these musical parodies, "postmodern carols," as they are not modern and... technically, they're not postmodern, either, but Da-da had to call them something. Feel free to substitute your own apt descriptor for this weird epoch we're wading through.

Where was Da-da?

Ah, yes. These are called "carols" as they're to be sung in a bright and spirited and annoyingly cheerful manner, usually on a street corner, the DMV, a gray cubicle, or amidst any public transportation setting. In this manner will all within earshot join in and sing as one. Or alert the authorities. Anyway, enjoy.

POSTMODERN CAROL #1
"CAROL OF THE SMOKED MEAT"

Da-da wrote this for all those dragging through the various holiday seasons. And since Da-da and Santa use the same surveillance systems, Da-da KNOWS what you need. Ready? Of course you are.

Ok, can there be anything more inspiring than Christmas carols about smoked meat? No, there can't. In this warped klieg-light, here's a festive *aperçus* into what A Man Called Da-da will soon be singing in your head. All day. You're welcome. Now, get out of bed, dress in red, put on your head, and inject cheer instead. And please don't rhyme, it's annoying. Anyway, SING you stylish, inebriated holiday apes, SING!

"CAROL OF THE SMOKED MEAT"
[sung to the tune of "Deck the Halls"]

Deck the halls with boughs of sausage,
Fa la la la la, la la la la.
Tis the season filled with costage,
Fa la la la la, la la la la.

Jump we now in bacon barrel,
Fa la la, la la la, la la la.
Troll the Ancient smoked meat carol,
Fa la la la la, la la la la.

See the blazing fool before us,
Fa la la la la, la la la la.
Strike the pork of loin some more-us.
Fa la la la la, la la la la.

Follow me in linky pleasure,
Fa la la la la, la la la la.
While I tell of drool-tide treasure,
Fa la la la la, la la la la.

Fast away the cold beer passes,
Fa la la la la, la la la la.
Hail the brew, ye lads and lasses,
Fa la la la la, la la la la.

Sing smoked sausage, all together,
Fa la la la la, la la la la.
Heedless of the health bellwether,
Fa la la la la, la la la la.

POSTMODERN CAROL #2
"SANTA CALLING"

Since The Clash would NEVER do a Christmas album, and since Da-da had this tune stuck in his head all day while wrapping presents... this postmodern parodic carol was born.

"SANTA CALLING"
[*Sung to "London Calling" w/ apologies to The Clash*]

Santa calling, to the faraway towns
Now Christmas declared, the sled's comin' down
Santa calling, from the Northern world
Come out of the naughty, you boys and girls
Santa calling, now don't cry or fuss
his list is all made, in Santa we trust
Santa calling, see we ain't got no ding
'Cept for the ching of that reindeer thing

[*chorus*]

The Nice age is comin', the sack's zoomin' in
touchdown expected, the house full of kin
The getting go running, but I have no fear
'Cause Santa is coming, and I know he'll deliver

Santa calling, to the gimme-tation zone
Forget it, brother, you can go it alone
Santa calling, to the kiddies of mess
Start cleanin' up, and do more with "Yes"
Santa calling, and you better not shout
you better not cry, and you better not pout
Santa calling, see he just ain't no lie
He's the one with the twinkly eye

[*chorus*]

The Nice age is coming, the sack's zoomin' in
touchdown expected, the house full of kin
A naughty/nice error, but I have no fear
'Cause Santa is coming, and I... I know he'll deliver!
Now get this:

Santa calling, yes, he does exist, too
An' you know what Da-da said? Well, some of it was true!
Santa calling, and he'll make it worthwhile
And after all this, won't you give him a smile?
Santa calling...

I never egged my nog so much so much [fading] so much so much...

POSTMODERN CAROL #3
"NOEL ERUCTATION"

Da-da wrote this way back in '86 when he was still a musician. It's basically "A Christmas Song" parodied in what Da-da calls, "The Roget Language," which will become as self-evident and annoying as everyone else found, "The Roget Language."

Here are the original lyrics:

"A CHRISTMAS SONG"
[by Mel Torme, The Velvet Fog]

Chestnuts roasting on an open fire,
Jack Frost nipping on your nose,
Yuletide carols being sung by a choir,
And folks dressed up like Eskimos.
Everybody knows a turkey and some mistletoe,
Help to make the season bright.
Tiny tots with their eyes all aglow,
Will find it hard to sleep tonight.
They know that Santa's on his way;
He's loaded lots of toys and goodies on his sleigh.
And every mother's child is going to spy,
To see if reindeer really know how to fly.
And so I'm offering this simple phrase,
To kids from one to ninety-two,
Although its been said many times, many ways,
Merry Christmas to you.

Now, here's the same thing (next page) in, "The Roget Language," invented by A Man Called Da-da way back when he was blissfully un-kid-laden and borderline sane. Note#1: Da-da has successfully sung this all he way through, without mistakes — and even recorded it — but only once, as it's near-impossible.

Note#2: "Abiotic-neuter-pronoun" is a fancy Roget way of saying, "it." Shows just how annoying "The Roget Language" really is, and that it was indeed written by a teenager.

"NOEL ERUCTATION"
[sung to "A Christmas Song" with apologies to The Velvet Fog]

Castanea-dentata progeny thermo-calefacting on a loculus flaming chasm;
Jacob Canescence ingesting ambiant proboscic cartilage;
Gothic Juleic arias effectively enunciated by a glee conglomeration,
And genraic-body-politic sheathed-adjacent-dimensional-vicinity, "eaters of raw meat."

Ceterus-parabus-gestalt-beings cognate, a meleagris gallopavo and viscum-album-arboreal parasites
Shall succor affecting capricious metamorphoses astronomic-canicular-finale-effulgent;
Exiguitous evanescent homunculoids combining-formulant-possessive oculi holistic-corpus-coruscating facula,
Shall espialate abiotic-neuter-pronoun inducta-lithoidically-obdurate to ostially-pandiculate-corpuscular-vespus post-meridian.

Convocative-biped-contingents abstrusely fathom that sanguine-inveterate-hoary-Seraphim-Nicholas' imminently coincidental-intrinsicalitous space-time-inclusion;
He's geotropically deposited ample post-infantic glee contrivances and nonfunctional garniture on his static pluviosity conveyance,
And ecumenic ova-secreter's animate-cell-conglomeration's evacuating post-respiratory miasma,
To scotopiacally photopiate if mammalian epidermis-controlled quadrapeds manifestly grasp aeronautical engineering principles.

And thus, I'm infeodatingly relegating this unadulterated

homogenaic reductivistic locution,
To juvanescent neonates from fused organic unity to nonage bifurcation;
Albeit abiotic-neuter-pronoun's existed phonemically-sequential vibration, multifarious temporal episodes, imminently rife procedures;
Jocular Savioral Anniversarial Womb-exit — to you.

POSTMODERN CAROL #4
"WE NEED A LITTLE BUSINESS"

In keeping with all postmodern sentences ostensibly beginning with a prepositional phrase... and ellipsed by what's become more of a holiday BUYING season than an historical, spiritual event... A Man Called Da-da penned this postmodern ditty, which has become the primary holiday theme song for the past XX decades.

"WE NEED A LITTLE BUSINESS"
[*sung to "We Need a Little Christmas" by Bronislau Kaper*]

Haul out the folly
Ramp up the fee before my spirit falls again
Sell off the stock please
I may be rushing things but, check the calls again now

For we need a little business
Right this very minute
Panic in the windows
(Fox) Carols that will spin it

Yes, we need a little business
Right this very minute
It hasn't snowed a single morning
But Santa, dear, it's global warming

So crank up the chintzy
Turn up the longest string of blights I've ever seen
E-lect the fruitcake
It's time we put some whack-O in that Oval Thing now

For I've grown a little meaner
Grown a little colder
Grown a little sadder
Grown a little bolder

And I need a little barcode
tattooed on my shoulder
I need a little business now!

For we need a little boozage
Need a little snoozage
Need a little flinging
bringing The Hereafter

And we need a little trashy
"Happy ever after"
We need a little business now!

POSTMODERN CAROL #5
"WOKE UP, IT WAS
A ZOMBIE MORNING"

Da-da wrote this for New Year's Day, 1-1-11, or "One One One One" as everyone said in the mental ward. If you're anything like Da-da (you couldn't possibly be that lucky), you went to bed at 9:00 pm and were up bright and early for a walk through the rye, drinking coffee and dodging errant zombies... er, neighbors, who'd been up all night running alcoholic reactors into the RED and looking a wee bit haggard that zombie morning.

"WOKE UP, IT WAS A ZOMBIE MORNING"
[sung to "Chelsea Morning" with apologies to Joni Mitchell]

Woke up, it was a ZOMBIE morning
And the first thing that I heard
Was a moan outside my window
And a dead thing wrote the words
It came wafting up like sick refrains
And something else like, "BRAAAAA-AINS"

Oh, won't you stay
We'll lock out the day
And wait 'till the army comes

Woke up, it was a ZOMBIE morning
And the first thing that I saw
Were dead arms through yellow curtains
And gruesome shadows on the wall
Red and dead and nasty welcome you
Crimson skull grins lean to beckon

Oh, won't you stay
We'll load up the day
There's a gun show every second

Now the curtain opens on a portrait of today
And the streets are paved with ZOMBIE
And religions fly
And papers lie
Waiting to blow you away

Woke up, it was a ZOMBIE morning
And the first thing that I knew
There was gore and hungry frenzy
And rolls of ammo belts, too
And the blood poured in like butterscotch
And stuck to my defenses

Oh, won't you stay
We'll rub out the day
And we'll talk in future tenses

When the blast door closes
And the survivors run away
I will feed your intense
Howls by night
By candlelight
By ghoul-light
If only you will stay
Pretty zombie, won't you
Wake up, it's a ZOMBIE morning…

The Tao of Da-da

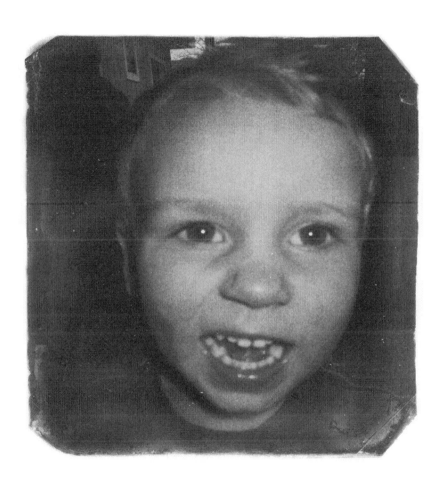

POSTMODERN CAROL #6
"EVERYONE KNOWS IT'S BATMAN"

Da-da's micro-progeny, Bronko & Nagurski, were rather BAT-manic for a time. And since Da-da is constantly plagued by various whammies dredged from a tragic childhood Top 40, we find ourselves dancing a spooky jig to a badly tuned station near a dimly lit crossroads full of... whatever this is.

"EVERYONE KNOWS IT'S BATMAN"
[sung to "Everyone Knows It's Windy" by The Association]

Who's standin' at the edge of a building
Calling a plane that's high in the air
Who's windin' up to give me a brain-blow
Everyone knows it's Bat-maan

Who's zoomin' down the streets of the city
Scowlin' at everybody he sees
Who's fightin' foes to erase a moment
Everyone knows it's Bat-maan

And Batman has spooky eyes
That flash at the sound of lies
And Batman has wings to fly
Above the clouds (above the clouds)
Above the crowds (above the crowds)

[bat-flute solo]

And Batman has spooky eyes
That flash at the sound of lies
And Batman has wings to fly
Above the clouds (above the clouds)
Above the crowds (above the crowds)

Who's grumpin' down the streets of the city
Sneerin' at everybody he sees
Who's sneakin' out to capture a Scarecrow
Everyone knows it's Bat-maan

Who's rackin' up defeats in the city
Conflicted by every cat-body he sees
Who's bendin' down to kick out a Two-face
Everyone knows it's Bat-maan

Who's stoppin' tricks and treats in the city
Unsmilin' at every riddle he sees
Who keeps revengin' up a lost-parent moment
Everyone knows it's Bat-maan

Who's rippin' up the freaks of the city
Smilin' at every body he sees
Who's ninja deck is dealin' a Joker
Everyone knows it's Bat-maan

Who's bitterness eclipses the city
Fighting with every insane Mr. Freeze
Who's vigilante meter's in foment
Everyone knows it's Bat-maan.

POSTMODERN CAROL #7
"THE SCHOOL BUS"

Frosty mornings redolent of diesel fumes, fear, and cheap hair products remind Da-da of his childhood. Da-da was one of those lucky kids forced to ride the school bus, long ago, in a township far far away. Like root canals, STDs, and bowling with your ex, the school bus was one of those childhood episodes you won't soon forget, but SO want to. Anyway, when Da-da wasn't being beaten by some bearded 11-year-old on said transport, he'd make fun of the songs the bus driver forced us to listen to, as if riding a gaseous old creaking mobile barn filled with equally gaseous and homicidal prepubescent inmates wasn't bad enough. Worse still, Da-da was forced *to play this song* during a Jr. High band concert. Believe Da-da, it was worse on our end.

"THE SCHOOL BUS"
[sung to "The Love Boat" with barest of apologies to Paul Williams and Charles Fox]

BUS... exciting and... pew!
Come aboard. We're expecting you!
And... BUS, that dreaded transport.
Let it smoke... it smokes back to you...

[hideous screech of brakes]

The SCHOO-OOL BUS... soon will be making another run
The SCHOO-OOL BUS... promises horror for everyone...
Get a course on butt-clencher,
You hide from some psycho's rants...

[driver yells, someone cries]

And **B U S**... will hurt evermore

[*red light horn honk riff*]

It's a broken smile... or a deadly snore.

[*tires sing on wet pavement*]

It's BU-UUUUUUUUUS!

Welcome aboard the SCHOO-OOOOL BUS!

POSTMODERN CAROL #8
"BINARY IN A CODE MINE"

Da-da once worked for a concert promotions unit, and one day, Gordon Sumner... er, STING took offense to Da-da reading STING's lyrics aloud backstage...

> Da-da [reading album notes]: "'*Gee, I hope my legs don't break, walking on the moon.*' Wow, that's inspired, Gordon."
> STING: "I needed one more song to pad out the album. And since I was walking around the hotel room... which was boring, I made it moon."
> Da-da: "That is so sad."
> STING: "You're fired."
> Da-da: "Thank you."

You all already knew this because you *love* STING. Who doesn't? What was Da-da saying? Oh. Da-da also used to work for several tech start-ups here and there, and found their culture SO appealing and memorable -- and their STING connection so... *je ne sais quoi* -- he thought the two should live together. Forever. This is for you, Gordo.

> **"BINARY IN A CODE MINE"**
> *[sung to "Canary in a Coal Mine" with apologies to Gordo]*
>
> First to fall over when your lines of code are less than perfect
> Your sensibilities are so shaken by the slightest defect
> You live your life coding binary in a code mine
> You get so dizzy just recoding a command line
>
> You say you want to go outside and feel the sunshine
> You're so afraid to leave your cube without a deadline
> You live your life coding binary in a code mine
> You get so dizzy even parsing in a straight line

Binary in a codemine
Binary in a codemine
Binary in a codemine

Now if I tell you that you're just a lame code monkey
You do your work but jeez your code is so dang clunky
You live your life coding binary in a code mine
You look so busy faux-encoding for some overtime

Binary in a codemine
Binary in a codemine
Binary in a codemine

First to fall over when your lines of code are less than prefect
Your sensibilities are so shaken by the slightest defect
You live your life coding binary in a code mine
You get so dizzy just decoding a command line.

POSTMODERN CAROL #9 "I'M TOO FUSSY (EXTENDED FUSS MIX)"

Da-da is a veteran of SO many tantrums — and not just his own. He is, of course, talking about OPT (Other People's Tantrums), which Da-da bravely endures to this day, through all the years of being Mr. Mom and sometimes Mrs. Mom, depending on which clothes came out of the dryer.

"I'M TOO FUSSY (EXTENDED FUSS MIX)"
[sung to "I'm Too Sexy" by Right Said Fred]

I'm too fussy to be loved too fussy to be loved
Don't you touch me

I'm too fussy for this shirt too fussy for this shirt
So fussy it hurts
And I'm WAY too fussy for the park too fussy for the park
New York and Bismark

And I'm too fussy for gelato too fussy for gelato,
I may need a Clamato
And I'm too fussy for your party
Too fussy for your party
No way I'm too farty

I'm a toddler you know what I mean
And I do my little fuss on the dad-walk
Yeah on the dad-walk on the dad-walk yeah
I make da-da cuss on the dad-walk

Oh, I'm too fussy for the car too fussy for the car
Too fussy by far
And I'm too fussy for this hat

Too fussy for this hat but it works on the cat
I'm a toddler you know what I mean
And I do my little SCREAM on the dad-walk
Yeah on the dad-walk on the dad-walk yeah
I EXPOSE my little butt on the dad-walk

I'm too fussy for my too fussy for my too fussy for my

'Cos I'm a toddler you know what I mean
And I do my little fuss on the dad-walk
Yeah on the dad-walk on the dad-walk yeah
I wag my little tush on the dad-walk

I'm too fussy for the cat too fussy for the cat
Poor pussy cat
I'm WAY too fussy for my grandpa too fussy for my grandpa
but here comes grandma

And I'm too fussy for this song.

POSTMODERN CAROL #10
"TURN AROUND, MONSTER"

Da-da's boys once saw an especially traumatic "Ultraman" episode where the rubberized monster occupying the role of ULTRAMAN PUNCHING BAG was atypically sad because it had been knocked out of the "Outer Zone" by a misguided government missile test. This always happens to Da-da, too. Anyway, once on earth, the monster behaved in a quite un-monster-like fashion: he cried and cried AND CRIED, sounding exactly like steel girders collapsing, for what seemed like hours, until scientists and Ultraman and viewers finally couldn't stand it any longer and got the monster back home. Phew. But before that, the monster aimlessly wandered the countryside, howling and forlorn. Bronko, Da-da's youngest, actually started to cry for the sad monster (it really was sad), or maybe it was because Bronko's ears hurt due to the terrible sound. This lead Da-da to…

"TURN AROUND, MONSTER (A BRUTAL HIGH-KICK TO THE HEART)"
[Sung to "Total Eclipse of the Heart" by Bonnie Tyler]

Turnaround, every now and then I get sucked
outta the Outer Zone and made to walk around on TV
Turnaround, every now and then I get
a little bit tired of the awful grinding sound of my tears
Turnaround, every now and then I get a
little bit nervous that Ultraman is gonna beat me again
Turnaround, every now and then I get a
little bit happy till I see the judge-y look in his eyes
Turnaround MONSTER, every now and
then I'm torn apart
Turnaround MONSTER, every now and
then I'm torn apart

Turnaround, every now and then I get a
little bit restless and dream about some monster payback
Turnaround, every now and then I get a
little bit stupid when I'm howling like a whacko on crack
Turnaround, every now and then I get a
little bit angry and I need to kick some silvery butt
Turnaround, every now and then I get a
little bit nervous when I think I look like I'm inside-out
Turnaround MONSTER, every now and
then I'm torn apart
Turnaround MONSTER, every now and
then I'm blown apart

And I don't need Ultraman tonight
Or I'll bleed now more than ever
Oh if you'll only be polite
I'll stop making this noise forever
And you'll only be making it right
Cause we're so wrong together
You can karate till the end of the line
Your glove is like a shadow on me all of the time
I don't know what to do and I'm always in the dark
I'm feeling like a scrambled egg being eaten by Karl Marx
I can't stop weeping tonight
Monstertherapy starts tonight
Monstertherapy starts tonight

Once upon a time I was floating in space
Now I'm only falling apart
Nothing I can do
A brutal high-kick to the heart
Once upon a time there was Outer Zone
Now only, "ha-ya!" in the dark
Nothing I can say
A savage high-kick to the heart

[*monster/steel girder instrumental*]

Turnaround fright eyes
Turnaround fright eyes
Turnaround, every now and then I know
I'll never be the monster you wanted me to be
Turnaround, every now and then I know
I'll always be the Monster who was destined to cry so much on TV
Turnaround, every now and then I know
there's no one in the universe as powerful and macho as you
Turnaround, every now and then I know
there's no way a skeleton can rule the earth like Boo-boo
Turnaround fright eyes, every now and
then I'm torn apart
Turnaround fright eyes, every now and
then I'm blown apart

And I don't need Ultraman tonight
Or I'll bleed now more than ever
Oh if you'll only be polite
I'll stop making this noise forever
And you'll only be making it right
Cause we're so wrong together
You can karate till the end of the line
Your glove is like a shadow on me all of the time
I don't know what to do and I'm always in the dark
I'm feeling like a scrambled egg being eaten by Karl Marx
I can't stop weeping tonight
Monstertherapy starts tonight
Monstertherapy starts tonight

Once upon a time I was floating in space
Now I'm only falling apart
Nothing I can do
A brutal high-kick to the heart
Once upon a time there was Outer Zone
Now only, "ha-ya!" in the dark
Nothing I can say
A savage high-kick to the heart.

POSTMODERN CAROL #11
"UFO IN THE BACKYARD"

In honor of Da-da's boys and friends having their own UFO flap, literally in the backyard, here's this. (Note: say, "YOUFO," and this works. Otherwise, you've got that extra syllable rankling around and the mothership will never take you back.)

"UFO IN THE BACKYARD"
[Sung to "MIRROR IN THE BATHROOM" by The English Beat]

UFO in the backyard
please take me
The door's unlocked
just you and me.
Can you take me to a planet
that's got mass tables
You can weigh the probe
while you are beeping.

UFO in the backyard
I just can't stop it,
Every day you see me
window stopping.
I find no interest in the
sad airwaves
Just a thousand reflections
of our Ancient self, self, self...

UFO in the backyard
You're my UFO in the backyard
You're my UFO in the backyard
You're my UFO in the backyard...

UFO in the backyard
recompense
For all my crimes
planetary defense.
Crop circle whispers
make no sense
Drifting gently into
mental illness.

UFO in the backyard
transport me
The door's unlocked
just you and me.
Can you take me to a planet
that's got mass tables
You can weigh my atoms
while you are sleeping.

UFO in the backyard
UFO in the backyard…

POSTMODERN CAROL #12
"(TALKIN' 'BOUT) MY EDUCATION"

Da-da went to a state college. Every day, we'd all run outside and yell, "STATE!" Yeah, didn't impress anyone then, either. Anyway, behold the new anthem for post-secondary education.

(Note: This postmodern carol got more hits on Da-da's blog than all other posts combined, which should tell you something — either about the current poor state of education today, or about just how lame Da-da's site really is.)

"(TALKIN' 'BOUT) MY EDUCATION"
[sung to "My Generation" with apologies to The WHO]

People try to put it d-down (Talkin' 'bout my education)
Just because I goofed around (Talkin' 'bout my education)
Things they do look awful c-c-cold (Talkin' 'bout my education)
Hope I'm employed before I get old (Talkin' 'bout my education)

This is my education
This is my education, baby

Why don't you all t-t-trade away (Talkin' 'bout my allegation)
And don't try to sell what we all s-s-say (Talkin' 'bout my condemnation)
I'm not trying to cause a big s-s-sensation (Talkin' 'bout my adaptation)
I'm just talkin' 'bout my ed-d-d-ducation (Talkin' 'bout my education)

This is my education
This is my education, baby

Why don't you m-m-masquerade away (Talkin' 'bout your obfuscation)
And don't try to b-buy what they all s-s-say (Talkin' 'bout my suffocation)
I'm not trying to cause a b-big s-s-sensation (Talkin' 'bout my demarcation)
I'm just talkin' 'bout my ed-d-d-ducation (Talkin' 'bout my education)

This is my education
This is my education, baby
People pepper spray us d-down (Talkin' 'bout my fumigation)
Just because we sit around (Talkin' 'bout my liberation)
Things they do look awful s-s-sold (Talkin' 'bout your corporation)
Yeah, hope I die before I'm controlled (Talkin' 'bout my education)

This is my education
This is my education, baby

The Tao of Da-da

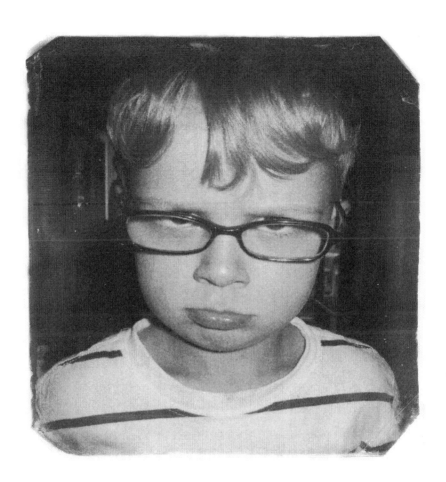

POSTMODERN CAROL #13 "BAD MALL SANTA DA-DA"

Sure, this sounds like a cross between a drunken R&B tune and a Grand Mal seizure, but just to prove to Da-da's mother-in-law that Da-da's not just any bum — *but an ENLIGHTENED BUM* (in the American *and* British sense) — Da-da signed up to play Santa at a local mall one holiday season, primarily because he already had the beard and the suit, and can automatically reference himself in the Third Person. Da-da's first tiny Yuletide victim was a 5-year-old miniature Harry Potter, who was a little too serious. Also note that the mall wanted Da-da to cover ALL the holiday bases, so "Merry Christmas!" became, "Merry Chris-kwanza-naka!" Anyway, here's what the kid said:

> Da-da: "What would you like for the holidays little boy?"
> Harry: "I want Rhodesia."
> Da-da: "W-what? You want what?" [Santa Da-da looked at the mom in attendance and she just shrugged.]
> Harry: "Rhodesia. I want it."
> Da-da: "Ok. Rhodesia. Santa's pretty sure it's called, 'Zimbabwe' now – which sounds better, and is equally unstable..."
> Harry: "I want it."
> Da-da: "And you shall have it, my little Idi Amin reincarnation. Merry Chris-kwanza-naka!"

Da-da gave the tyke a sugar-free, low-residue, high protein kelp "kane" and reached for the bourbon in Santa's sack. Here's the song that was stuck in Da-da's head nearly every day of this jocular yuletide experience.

"BAD MALL SANTA DA-DA"
[*Sung to "Sweet Home Alabama" by Lynyrd Skynyrd, who's got way too many consonants in his name*]

Big sleigh keep on burnin'
Sit me down to save my skin
Playing Santa in the Voidlands
I miss my brain once again
And I think its all in, yes

Well I heard Mrs. Santa yell about it
Well, I heard ol' Gramma put it down
Well, I hope Bronko will remember
A Bad Mall Santa knows no fear

Bad Mall Santa Da-da
Where the faces are so blue
Bad Mall Santa Da-da
Dude, I'm barfing onto you

In Santa Lands they love the toy box
Now we all did what we could do
Now givin' toys don't bother Santa
Does your conscience bother you?
Tell the truth

Bad Mall Santa Da-da
Where the faces are so blue
Bad Mall Santa Da-da
Dude, I'm barfing onto you
Here comes lunch, Santa

Now the Disney Lands got the Weirdos
And they've been known to bring a kid or two
Dude they scare Santa so much
They stick in pins when he's feelin' blue
Now how about you?

Bad Mall Santa Da-da
Where the faces are so blue
Bad Mall Santa Da-da
Dude, I'm barfing onto you

Bad Mall Santa Da-da
Oh sweet Da-da baby
Where the faces are so blue
And Mall Security's so true

Bad Mall Santa Da-da
Dude
Dude, I'm barfing onto you
Yeah, Santa Da-da's got the answer.

POSTMODERN CAROL #14
"THE TIME-OUT"

After one particularly prolonged and drawn out squawk of a week, combined with several four-alarm no-holds-barred grudge matches between Da-da's boys, Da-da had to enforce multiple time-outs that still seem to echo forever. Needless to say, this was bouncing around in Da-da's big ol' empty head all day, every day.

"THE TIME-OUT"
[*Sung to "TIME WARP" from "Rocky Horror Picture Show"*]

It's astounding, Time-Outs fleeting
Madness takes its toll
But listen closely, not for very much longer
Da-da's got to take control
Da-da remembers giving the Time-Out
Drinking during moments when
The tantrum would hit and Freud would be calling

Let's do that Time-Out again...
Let's give that Time-Out again!

It's just a sit on the left
And then a sit on the right
With your brain full-eclipse
You squinch your eyes down tight
But it's the ironic thrust that really drives you insane,
Let's do that Time-Out again!

You're so screamy, O fantasy free me!
No one wants to BE me, no not at all
In another dimension, with inelastic attention
Undeluded, Da-da sees all
In a bit of a mind flip
You induced brother's stair slip

And nothing will ever be the same
Your spaced out aberration, like your brain's on vacation!

Let's do that Time-Out again!

Sure you were sittin in your seat just a-havin a think
When your brother did something set you over the brink
He shook you up, he took you by surprise
He had your fire truck and the devil's eyes.
He stared at you and you felt a change
You whacked him in the head, you'd never do it again (but)

Let's do that Time-Out again!

It's just a sit on the left
And then a sit on the right
With your brain full eclipse
You squinch your eyes down tight
But it's the ironic thrust that really drives you insane

Let's do that Time-Out again...
Let's give that Time-Out again!

POSTMODERN CAROL #15
"WE ARE JANE CAMPION"

No one believes this story. It's mostly true. Da-da was guesting at a writers' workshop and to warm folks up, he asked those assembled to name some of their writing inspirations. People muttered amongst themselves and called out various names of writers, filmmakers, poets, fast food mascots, etc. Strangely, the entire front row — consisting of four elderly ladies dressed as Santa Claus — spoke amongst themselves a moment before reaching a consensus, and blurting out in unison: "We are Jane Campion."

This simple declarative sentence fired all 998 cylinders of Da-da's Satirical Tourette's Syndrome (not to be confused with Da-da's Shakespearean Tourette's Syndrome), making Da-da fairly vibrate for a second as he tried to overcome these natural urges. He failed, grabbed the microphone and broke into song. Other people picked it up, and soon the whole room was singing, *much to the confusion of bookstore staff and passersby* – not to mention the local police who had to break it up. Here's what we all sang (well, the chorus, anyway):

"WE ARE JANE CAMPION"
[*Sung to "WE ARE THE CHAMPIONS" by Freddie Mercury*]

I've paid my dues
Time after time
I've done this sentence
But committed no rhyme
And bad mistakes
I've made a few
I've had my share of syntax
Kicked in my face
But I've come through

'Cause we mean to write on and on and on

WEEEEE ARE JANE CAMPION, MY FRIENDS
WE'LL GO ON WRITING TILL THE END
WE ARE JANE CAMPION
WE ARE JANE CAMPION
NO TIME FOR BOOZERS
CAUSE WE ARE JANE CAMPIONS... OF THE WORLD!

I've taken my prose
And my uncertain scrawls
It's brought me misfortune
And everything that goes with it
I thank you all
Sure it's no pop apotheosis
Not without the muse
I consider it a challenge before
The whole bloomin' place
That I ain't gonna booze

'Cause we mean to write on and on and on and on

WEEEEE ARE JANE CAMPION, MY FRIENDS
WE'LL GO ON WRITING TILL THE END
WE ARE JANE CAMPION
WE ARE JANE CAMPION
NO TIME FOR BOOZERS
CAUSE WE ARE JANE CAMPIONS... OF THE WORLD!

WEEEEE ARE JANE CAMPION, MY FRIENDS
WE'LL GO ON WRITING TILL THE END
WE ARE JANE CAMPION!
WE ARE JANE CAMPION!
NO TIME FOR BOOZERS
CAUSE WE ARE JANE CAMPIONS... OF THE WORLD!

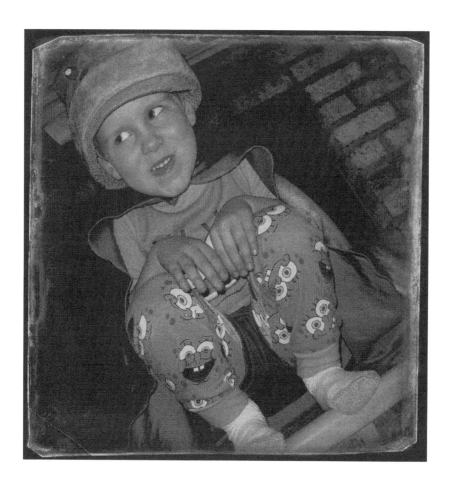

POSTMODERN CAROL #16
"GET YER BUTT IN YER SEAT"

Da-da's youngest, Bronko, *cannot* sit in his seat at mealtime. Da-da's tried everything short of duct-tape. Nothing works. Without further ado, this is what Da-da sings nearly every night.

"GET YER BUTT IN YER SEAT"
[*Sung to "TAKIN' IT TO THE STREETS" with apologies to Michael McDonald and the Doobie Brothers*]

Get that cheesecake off your brother
It doesn't look good in his hair
Your ears don't work too well in this world
Fairly soon your crimes will tell.

Now You, yellin' 'bout the things you're gonna do to me
I ain't blind and I don't like what I think I see
Get your butt in yer seat
Chain your butt to that seat
Get your butt in yer seat
Get your butt to that seat

Take this message to your brother
you will find him in underwear
Whenever you boys eat together
You need be chained to a chair.

Now You, yellin' 'bout some things you saw on the TV
I'm half blind because I'm tired of what I know I see
Get your butt in yer seat
Chain your butt to that seat
Get your butt in yer seat
Get your butt to that seat

Take your message to your mother

tell her Da-da is unfair
Whenever you guys are together
You make Da-da yell and swear

Now You, howlin' like a freakin' little butt-banshee
I'm unkind and I don't care what you think of me (but)
Get your butt in yer seat
Chain your butt to that seat
Get your butt in yer seat
Get your butt to that seat

Get your butt in yer seat
Chain your butt to that seat
Get your butt in yer seat
Get your butt to that seat

POSTMODERN CAROL #17
"KEEP US IN LINE"

Da-da wrote this after he read about Penn State banning Neil Diamond's, "Sweet Caroline," from being sung at football games (punishment or reprieve?), so Da-da OF COURSE got the stupid song stuck in his head: *whammied, not stirred*. To purge this dirge, Da-da drew on recent Piranha Brother behavior, with the below tune meant to feature the boys singing to Da-da, but since singing requires one to stop pummeling one's brother, it's probably not gonna happen anytime soon. Now that you know the backstory, please note that Da-da's added onomotopoetic sound effects [IN BRACKETS] because he's just that way.

"KEEP US IN LINE"
[*Sung to "Sweet Caroline" by Neil Diamond*]

How we began,
our bad behavior growin'
and don't you know it's grown in STRONG
tying that thing
around the bathroom door knob
Who'd have believed we'd go so wrong.

Bands, rubber bands
Reachin' out, touchin' pee... touchin' poo!
KEEP US IN LINE [BUMP BUMP BUMM]
we never do the things we should
we've been inclined [WHUMP BUMP NUMB]
to do the things you never would...
but now we, hide out of sight
'cause Da-da's face is scary
we didn't mean to use so much glue.

Sorry you hurt,
we couldn't stop the boulders

we thought that you both knew kung fu
Warm, squishy form
Reachin' out, slimin' me... slimin' you!
KEEP US IN LINE [JUMP BUMP BUMM]
we never do the things we should
we've been inclined
to do the things you never would
Oh, no, no

KEEP US IN LINE [THUMP BUMP NUMB]
we never do the things we should
KEEP US IN LINE [BUMP WHUMP DUNG]
our heads aren't really made of wood
KEEP US IN LINE...

POSTMODERN CAROL #18
"YODA UNDERPANTS"

At Chez Da-da (aka, "House-O-Da-da," aka, "Da-da-ville," aka, "Shutupandgetonwithit"), one is allowed one present on Christmas Eve, typically a gag gift. One year's silly giftage for the boys was a huge hit: Yoda underpants. Then-5YO Bronko and 7YO Nagurski immediately took off all their clothes and donned their new underpants — right in front of all assembled — and danced all over the place like half-naked mental patients... which of course they are. This gave Da-da the idea for post-postmodern parenting carol #19.

"YODA UNDERPANTS"
[*Sung to "Safety Dance" by Men Without Pants... er, Hats*]

Y-y-y-y O-o-o-o D-d-d-d A-a-a-a Y-o-d-a-a-a-a-a
Under, pants!

[Spoken]
You can prance if you want to
You can leave your pants behind
'Cause when friends all dance in Yoda underpants
Then they're all friends of mine
I say, you can wear what you want to
Underpants that'll make 'em blind
And we can act like we come from out of this world
Leave the real world far behind
With underpants

[Sung]
You can prance if you want to
You can leave your pants behind
'Cause our friends all dance in Yoda underpants
and they're all friends of mine

I say, you can wear what you want to
underpants that'll make 'em blind
And we can act like we come from out of this world
Leave the real world far behind
With underpants
Underpants!

We can show what we want to
The Yoda-tights are gonna fly
And we can fess complete with green butts in the street
Then ignore it like we're in Mumbai
Say, "Underpants" if you want to
If you don't nobody will
And you can act half-nude and totally imbued
And I can act like an imbecile

[Refrain]
I say, underpants, underpants
Everybody outta control
Underpants, underpants
They're wearin' 'em from pole to pole
Underpants, underpants
Everybody cover your glands
Underpants, underpants
Everybody takin' the cha-a-a-ance

With their underpants
Yoda underpants
Yoda underpants

Y-y-y-y O-o-o-o D-d-d-d A-a-a-a
Under, pants!

Take off your pants if you want to
Jump around and twirl in time
As long as we abuse it we're never gonna lose it
Everything is gonna work out fine
I say, you can prance if you want to

You can leave your pants behind
'Cause your friends all dance in their underpants
which makes 'em all friends of mine

[Refrain]

Yoda underpants, Yoda underpants, oh Yoda underpants [6x]
Yoda Underpants

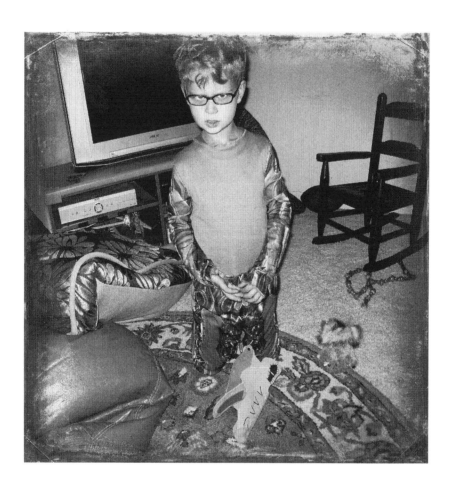

POSTMODERN CAROL #19
"LET IT GO"

Here's some music to forgive by, inspired by Da-da's boys who seem constantly at each others' throats. It was also written for Da-da's bro, Gary Renard, who was having a birthday at the time.

"LET IT GO"
[*sung to "Let It Snow"*]

Oh your brother outside is frightful
And your ire is not delightful
But since we've no place to go
Let It Go! Let It Go! Let It Go!

It's finally showin' signs of stoppin'
So I've bought some corn for poppin'
The slights are turned way down low
Let It Go! Let It Go! Let It Go!

When we finally dismiss the fight
How that date will abolish the storm
But if you'll really behold me bright
All the way home we'll be warm

O the universe is slowly dyin'
And, my dear, we're done goodbyin'
As long as you love me so
Let It Go! Let It Go! Let It Go!

POSTMODERN CAROL #20 "INCONCEIVABLE"

Da-da was watching one of his favorite movies when this popped into his head. It seemed to aptly describe most children and governments on earth — as well as anything having to do with the dread pirate Roberts, swordsmen, giants, and the Cliffs of Insanity.

"INCONCEIVABLE"
[*sung to "Unforgettable" by Nat King Cole, a merry old soul*]

Inconceivable, that's what you are
Inconceivable, though near or far
Like a song of, "HUH?" that clings to me
How parenthood does things to me
Never before has something been more

Inconceivable, in every way
And forever more, that's how we'll stay
That's why, darling, it's incredible
That something so irrepressible
Can be so reprehensible, too.

Inconceivable, in every way
And forever more, that's how we'll stay
That's why, darling, it's incredible
That something so indefensible
Can be so repeating decimal, too.

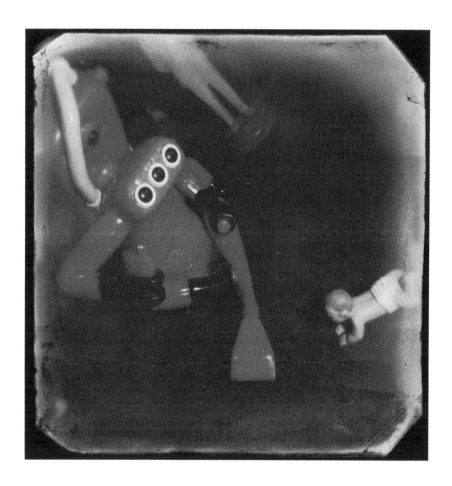

POSTMODERN CAROL #21
"POLICE ROBOT"

Since a new form of futuristic law enforcement is coming soon to a mall near you, Da-da figured it was special enough to warrant its own theme song.

"POLICE ROBOT"
[*Sung to the tune of "Pretty Woman" by Mr. Orbison*]

Police robot, walking down the street
Police robot, impervious to heat
Police robot, I don't believe you,
you're not the truth
No one could act as good as you... Murphy

Police robot, won't you pardon me?
Police robot, I couldn't help but see
Police robot, you look almighty as can be
Are you lonely just like me?
Police robot, stop awhile

Police robot, talk awhile
Police robot, waive that trial for me

Police robot, yeah, yeah, yeah
Police robot, look away
Police robot, say you'll not slay me
'Cause I fear you, I'll treat you right
Stay away, cyborg, jug wine tonight

Police robot, just walk on by
Police robot, don't make me cry
Police robot, just walk away, hey, okay
If that's the way it must be, okay

I guess I'll go on home, it's late
There'll be tomorrow night, but wait
What do I see?
Is he walking back to me
Yeah, he's walking back to me
Oh, no, police robot
Police robot, just walk on by
Police robot, don't make me cry
Police robot, just walk away, hey, okay

POSTMODERN CAROL #22
"THAT'S INFOTAINMENT"

Da-da has no idea where this came from. Like an infotainment commercial itself, does it matter? For whatever reason, this song stuck itself in his brain like a fish on a stick... which is not only a lovely image, but also indicative of parenthood and many an infotainment demonstration. This carol also owns title to being one of the toughest songs to parody while maintaining meter, but that's not your problem, that's... INFOTAINMENT!

"THAT'S INFOTAINMENT!"
[*sung to "That's Entertainment." On purpose.*]

The gown with the 'mazing markdown
Or the pants that make you dream of romance
Or the scene where the clothes all come clean!
That's infotainment!

The lights on the low purchase price
Or the bride with the bra extra wide
Or the doll that really gives it her all!
That's infotainment!

That hair-knot overwrought is simply teeming with sex
On a gay divorcee who really uses Bowflex
To develop T-Rex pecs
While a guy's playing soccer
As he oozes Oz-blue blocker

The jerk pretends to have too much work
And the boss who is thrown for a loss
By the skirt who is rubbing out dirt!

The world is a store,
The store is a world of infotainment.

That's infotainment!
That's infotainment!

The doubt after the jury is out
Or the thrill when they're buying the shill
Or the chase for the **font in boldface**!
That's infotainment!

The claim made by folks with no shame
Of the thing made by slaves in Beijing
With a shape
That makes you look like an ape!
That's infotainment!

It might be a sleight where the clothes all come clean
With bubbles tackling rubble from a greasy machine
Some great legal use of chlorobenzene
Described with a downbeat
By stars from "21 Jump Street"

The brag may be waving the flag
That's for sale even when he's in jail
Hip hooray!
The American way!
The world is a store
The store is a world of infotainment!

[

AFTERWORD

This textage was lovingly typeset in CasablancaAntique and MinionPro. Both seemed appropriate, but only because the dragon wasn't ready for his close-up. Please also note that all photographs are original works by Gary Clemenceau — except for the photo on p126, Bronko took that one — also except for any parodic, transformative pieces derived from public domain images. A limited run of select images is available at various sizes in an archival aluminum/polycarbonate matrix. Void where prohibited.

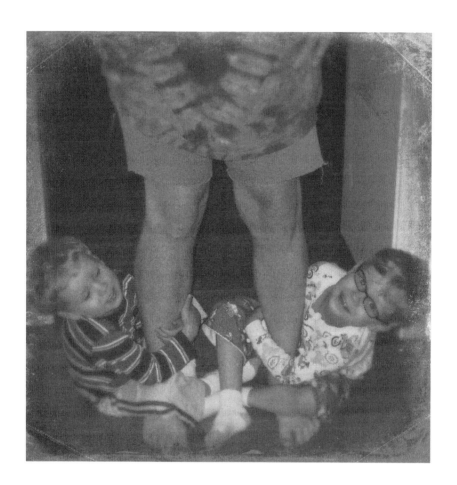

About the Author

Gary Clemenceau is an author, artist and photographer living in Northern California with his two sons, Bronko & Nagurski, and a very patient wife who has mostly stopped calling him names since her two deliveries. *TAO* is his third book.

For those wishing for more Da-da, please visit Da-da's singular blog at:

www.amancalleddada.com

Made in the USA
San Bernardino, CA
15 June 2015